The Black Archive #12

PYRAMIDS OF MARS

GW00481891

By Kate Orman

Published in 2017 by Obverse Books

Cover Design © Cody Schell

Text © Kate Orman

Kate would like to thank:

Kyla Ward and Q

For their invaluable feedback

Also Available

The Black Archive #1: Rose by Jon Arnold
The Black Archive #2: The Massacre by James Cooray Smith
The Black Archive #3: The Ambassadors of Death by LM Myles
The Black Archive #4: Dark Water / Death in Heaven by Philip
  Purser-Hallard
The Black Archive #5: Image of the Fendahl by Simon Bucher-Jones
The Black Archive #6: Ghost Light by Jonathan Dennis
The Black Archive #7: The Mind Robber by Andrew Hickey
The Black Archive #8: Black Orchid by Ian Millsted
The Black Archive #9: The God Complex by Paul Driscoll
The Black Archive #10: Scream of the Shalka by Jon Arnold
The Black Archive #11: The Evil of the Daleks by Simon Guerrier

Coming Soon

The Black Archive #13: Human Nature / The Family of Blood by
  Naomi Jacobs and Philip Purser-Hallard
The Black Archive #14: The Ultimate Foe by James Cooray Smith
The Black Archive #15: Carnival of Monsters by Ian Potter
The Black Archive #16: The Twin Dilemma by Gordon Ridout
The Black Archive #17: Full Circle by John Toon
The Black Archive #18: Marco Polo by Dene October
The Black Archive #19: The Impossible Planet / The Satan Pit by
  Simon Bucher-Jones
The Black Archive #20: Face the Raven by Sarah Groenewegen
The Black Archive #21: Heaven Sent by Kara Dennison
The Black Archive #22: Hell Bent by Alyssa Franke
The Black Archive #23: The Curse of Fenric by Una McCormack
The Black Archive #24: The Time Warrior by Matthew Kilburn
The Black Archive #25: Doctor Who (1996) by Paul Driscoll
The Black Archive #26: The Dæmons by Matt Barber

CONTENTS

OVERVIEW

Serial Title: *Pyramids of Mars*

Writer: Stephen Harris (Robert Holmes and Lewis Greifer)

Director: Paddy Russell

Original UK Transmission Dates: 25 October – 15 November 1975

Running Time: Episode 1: 25m 24s

Episode 2: 23m 55s

Episode 3: 24m 33s

Episode 4: 24m 42s

UK Viewing Figures: Episode 1: 10.5 million

Episode 2: 11.3 million

Episode 3: 9.4 million

Episode 4: 11.7 million

Regular cast: Tom Baker (Doctor Who), Elisabeth Sladen (Sarah Jane Smith)

Guest Cast: Bernard Archard (Marcus Scarman), Michael Sheard (Laurence Scarman), Peter Copley (Dr Warlock), Peter Mayock (Namin), Michael Bilton (Collins), Vik Tablian (Ahmed), Nick Burnell, Melvyn Bedford, Kevin Selway (Mummies), George Tovey (Ernie Clements), Gabriel Woolf (Sutekh)

Antagonists: Marcus Scarman, Sutekh

Novelisation: *Doctor Who and the Pyramids of Mars* by Terrance Dicks. **The Target Doctor Who Library** #50.

Sequels and Prequels: 'Scarab of Death' (short story, 1994), 'The Curse of the Scarab' (comic, 1995), *The Sands of Time* (novel, 1996), *GodEngine* (novel, 1996), 'The Power of Thoueris!' (comic, 2003), **The True History of Faction Paradox** (audio series, 2005-09), *The Bride of Peladon* (audio, 2008), *Transmission from Mars* (webcast, 2015), **The New Adventures of Bernice Summerfield:** *The Triumph of Sutekh* (audio series, 2015), **The Tenth Doctor** (comic series, 2015-).

Responses:

'*Pyramids of Mars*, with its claustrophobic atmosphere, judicious use of location filming, and strong performances from a small (and rapidly dwindling) cast, is regarded as a high point in [**Doctor Who**'s] history, representing the quintessence of earth-bound stories.'

[John J Johnston, 'Doctor Who: Pyramids of Mars' in *Mummies around the Word: An Encyclopedia of Mummies in History, Religion and Popular Culture*]

'A villain who spends the entire story sat immobile on a chair, a tiny cast of clichéd characters, plot holes big enough to drop a pyramid into, and a rubbish final episode, *Pyramids of Mars* is grossly overrated.'

[Mark Campbell, *The Pocket Essential Doctor Who*, p49]

SYNOPSIS

Episode 1

In Egypt in 1911, over the protests of his local helpers, archaeologist **Marcus Scarman** enters a sealed tomb from the First Dynasty, and is immediately struck down. An Egyptian named **Namin** takes up residence at the Priory, Marcus's family home in England, bringing with him an extensive collection of relics. When Marcus's friend **Dr Warlock** comes to confront the suspicious foreigner, Namin tries to kill him, but is prevented by the arrival of **the Doctor** and **Sarah**, diverted en route to UNIT headquarters – which will later stand on the Priory's site – by alien interference with the TARDIS.

The Doctor and Sarah rescue the wounded Warlock from Namin and his servants – walking **mummies** which have already killed Marcus's butler **Collins** – and take him to the Priory's Lodge, home of **Laurence Scarman**, Marcus's brother. Laurence has invented a rudimentary radio telescope which has detected a signal from Mars. The Doctor decodes it as 'Beware **Sutekh**' – apparently a reference to the Egyptian god Set.

At the Priory, Namin awaits the arrival of Sutekh himself through a time-space tunnel that opens inside a sarcophagus – but the space-suited figure which emerges identifies itself as merely Sutekh's servant. The Doctor, Sarah and Laurence, who have returned to the house, watch as it kills the now redundant Namin.

Episode 2

The newcomer is Marcus Scarman, co-opted as an animated cadaver by Sutekh. The god is in fact a renegade from the extraterrestrial Osiran civilisation on which pharaonic Egypt patterned itself. He was shut in a tomb by his brother Horus and his allies, imprisoned by a forcefield controlled from a pyramid on Mars. The control pyramid has been broadcasting a warning signal since Marcus's excavation lent Sutekh the possibility of escape.

The Doctor investigates the sarcophagus – the source of the interference in the TARDIS – but triggers a booby-trap. Meanwhile, the mummies – in fact Osiran service robots – establish an invisible barrier around the Priory. A poacher, **Ernie Clements**, is trapped in the grounds. He overhears as Marcus visits the Lodge and murders Warlock. Clements follows Marcus to the house and shoots him with his shotgun. Marcus's injuries immediately reverse themselves, and he dispatches two mummies to kill Clements.

The Doctor, Sarah and Laurence watch as other mummies unpack Namin's crates, revealing the components for an Osiran interplanetary missile which can destroy the control pyramid. Taking the ring with which Namin controlled the mummies, they retreat into the TARDIS, where Sarah suggests that they leave immediately. Briefly the Doctor shows her the current state of Earth in 1980: a dead world, blighted when they failed to defeat Sutekh in 1911. Returning, they go back to the Lodge, where the Doctor tries to convert Laurence's radio telescope into a device that will block Sutekh's mental control and free Marcus to die. Failing to understand that his brother is already dead, Laurence prevents its activation, even while mummies attack the Lodge.

Episode 3

In the struggle, one mummy destroys the machine and itself, but Sarah uses Namin's control ring to order the other one back to the

Priory. Leaving Laurence to unwrap the inert servicer robot, the Doctor and Sarah retrieve the gelignite Clements used for fishing. This involves deactivating part of the deflection barrier, which informs Sutekh that an extraterrestrial intelligence is opposing him.

Marcus visits the Lodge again. Though he remembers his brother, Sutekh's control of him is unbreakable, and he murders Laurence.

Disguised in the service robot's bandages, the Doctor plants the gelignite on the missile platform. Sarah triggers it with a bullet from Laurence's hunting-rifle, but Sutekh contains the explosion psychokinetically. The Doctor travels to Sutekh's tomb via the time-space tunnel and breaks the god's concentration. The missile is blown up, but the Doctor is Sutekh's prisoner.

Episode 4

The enthroned god's psychic powers make short work of the defiant Doctor, who is soon under his control. Sutekh dispatches him in the TARDIS with Marcus, a mummy, and Sarah as a hostage, to the Osiran pyramid on Mars. On arrival the service robot strangles the Doctor, but his Time Lord physiology enables him to survive. He and Sarah follow Marcus through various traps and logic puzzles to the heart of the pyramid, where Marcus channels Sutekh's power to destroy the controlling Eye of Horus. Sutekh withdraws his control from Marcus, who collapses into ash.

Realising that they have two minutes' grace before the lightspeed signal from Mars ceases to reach Earth, the Doctor and Sarah rush back to the Priory. They use the TARDIS's time controller to sabotage the time portal which Sutekh is using to travel from Egypt to England, ageing him to death. The sarcophagus explodes and the Doctor and Sarah leave the Priory to burn.

'AN EXCELLENT YEAR. ONE OF MY FAVOURITES.'

Why is *Pyramids of Mars* (1975) set in 1911? Lewis Greifer's original story outline was set in the near future of UNIT[1], but script editor Robert Holmes[2] pointed out a problem in that the Egyptian government no longer permitted the export of antiquities[3]. But why not place *Pyramids* in the Victorian era, when Britain's Egyptomania was at its height – the setting of two of the Hammer horror movies which inspired it? Alternatively, why not locate the story in the early 1920s, when the discovery of King Tutankhamun's 'absolutely untouched' tomb[4] triggered a new wave of obsession with mummies and curses?

In a way, *Pyramids* isn't set in 1911 at all; there are no references to historical events of the time. It was a comparatively quiet year in the history of Britain and the world. Perhaps this is not a fixed point in time, so Earth's history is vulnerable to Sutekh's vengeance[5]. An early 20th-century setting helps make Laurence Scarman's precocious invention of radio astronomy more plausible, lending

---

[1] Pixley, Andrew, 'Archive: Pyramids of Mars'. *Doctor Who Magazine* (DWM) #300, p33.
[2] When Griefer's scripts proved unusable, Holmes rewrote the story from scratch, retaining only some elements from Griefer's original outline (Pixley, 'Archive', p29).
[3] Pixley, 'Archive', p28.
[4] Marcus Scarman, *Pyramids of Mars* episode 1.
[5] This distinction was established in *The Waters of Mars* (2009). Or perhaps this **is** a fixed point, in some way only a Time Lord can see? After all, the Doctor says that what's taking place is 'contrary to the laws of the universe' (*Pyramids of Mars* episode 1).

the story an extra scientific element. (Sarah describes the repeated message from Mars as being '[l]ike an SOS'[6] – a shipping distress signal which had only recently come into international use, in 1908.)

The Talons of Weng-Chiang (1977) is *Pyramids'* fraternal twin – even closer than its other sibling story, *The Tomb of the Cybermen* (1967). As well as having the fourth Doctor, Robert Holmes, period settings, and false gods in common, both *Pyramids* and *Talons* are based on recent movie versions of period fiction about the mysterious, deadly East. Is there some connection between the Edwardian setting of *Pyramids* and the Victorian setting of *Talons*? The latter draws heavily on the Hallam Productions / Constantin Film **Fu Manchu** movies of the 1960s, but Fu is not a Victorian villain; he made his first appearance in a 1913 novel[7], most of the books were published in the 30s, and the 60s flicks were all set in the early 20th century. Perhaps Robert Holmes was saving the period for a full pastiche of 'the popular concept of Victoriana' – 'fog, gas lamps, hansom cabs, music halls'[8] – which couldn't have been fitted into *Pyramids'* small-scale, claustrophobic country-house setting.

My guess is that the year is a compromise between the 1890s and the 1920s, giving the story a look which, from the distant vantage point of the 1970s, loosely suggests both. Conveniently – so conveniently that it intrudes – Sarah is wearing a period-appropriate frock, described in the script as 'a faintly Edwardian

---

[6] Episode 1.
[7] In Rohmer, Sax, *The Mystery of Dr Fu-Manchu*.
[8] Russell, Gary, 'Interview: Robert Holmes'. DWM #100.

dress'[9]. Stargrove, the manor house in Hampshire whose exterior and grounds were used for location filming, was built in 1848[10], so it would suit any period setting after that[11].

By this point, you may be wondering why I have opened an essay on *Pyramids of Mars* with the minor issue of its period setting. That question has allowed me to introduce most of the subjects I'm going to discuss: the Hammer movies which the story pastiches; archaeology and the Egyptomania of the Victorian era and the 1920s; and the imperial fear of 'reverse colonisation'. I'll return to each of these, but for now, it's time to move on to another subject: Ancient Egypt and its mythology.

---

[9] Pixley, 'Archive', p30.
[10] Hampshire Gardens Trust.'Stargrove'.
[11] Including the contemporary setting of *Image of the Fendahl* (1977), also shot there. Barnes, Alan. 'The Fact of Fiction: Image of the Fendahl'. DWM #379, p43.)

'BEWARE SUTEKH'

Ancient Egypt's history begins a little over 5,000 years ago with the unification of Upper and Lower Egypt[12]. The Ancient Egyptians called their country 'The Two Lands'. Other names included 'the Black Land', where the annual flooding of the Nile deposited dark, fertile soil in which the Egyptians planted their crops, by contrast with the surrounding 'Red Land', the rocky desert[13]. At different times, Egypt's neighbours included Assyria, Persia, the Hittite Empire, and historical Palestine and Syria to the north-east; Nubia to the south; and ancient Libya to the west.

Scholars divide Egypt's 3,000 year history into six major periods:

- The Early Dynastic Period – the first two dynasties of the pharaohs.
- The Old Kingdom, when the pyramids were built.
- The Middle Kingdom.
- The New Kingdom, when well-known pharaohs such as Hatshepsut, Tutankhamun, and Ramesses the Great ruled.
- The Late Period.
- The Ptolemaic era, which ended with the death of Egypt's final pharaoh, Cleopatra VII, and Roman conquest[14].

---

[12] Upper Egypt is in the south, at a higher altitude.
[13] Lacovara, Peter, *The World of Ancient Egypt: A Daily Life Encyclopedia*, p428.
[14] Haywood, John, *The Penguin Historical Atlas of Ancient Civilizations*, p55.

Egypt remained a province of Rome for centuries[15]. After changing hands many times, the country became part of the Ottoman Empire in 1571.

Fitting the Osirans' visit to Earth into Egypt's history is a little tricky. The Doctor says that Sutekh has been trapped for 7,000 years[16]; if so, the Osirans were in Egypt during its Neolithic period, centuries before recognisable Ancient Egyptian culture began to appear. Robert Holmes' intention is clearly that the Osirans inspired Ancient Egyptian architecture, state religion, and culture; he places Sutekh's 'tomb' in Saqqara, near those of many of Egypt's earliest pharaohs, and Marcus Scarman dates it to the First Dynasty[17].

On the other hand, the vestibule of the tomb is painted with scenes from the tomb of Queen Nefertari and contains a copy of Tutankhamun's chair – both members of New Kingdom royalty, from more than a millennium later. One of the sarcophagi stored at the Scarman house is a crude but recognisable copy of the gilded outer coffin of Henutmehyt, a priestess from the New Kingdom, on display at the British Museum[18]. Perhaps some of Sutekh's worshippers did a bit of redecorating, and left offerings for their god? After all, in the centuries after his burial, Tutankhamun's tomb was broken into and items stolen or damaged, but the tomb was then officially resealed and reburied[19].

---

[15] Shaw, Ian, *The Oxford History of Ancient Egypt*.
[16] Episode 2.
[17] Episodes 2, 1.
[18] 'Gilded Outer Coffin of Henutmehyt'. British Museum.
[19] Edwards, IES, *Tutankhamun, His Tomb and Its Treasures*.

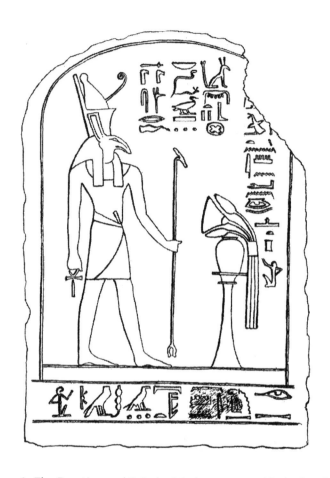

Figure 1: *The Egyptian god Set, depicted as a man with the head of the Set-animal (the square-eared, long-tailed creature visible in the hieroglyphs at top right), wearing the double crown of a pharaoh. A stela from Set's temple in Nubt (modern Kom Ombo).*[20]

---

[20] From Plate LXXVIII in Petrie, WM Flinders, and JE Quibell, *Naqada and Ballas.*

'What Do You Know of Sutekh?'

'Sutekh' is one of several variations of the name of the Ancient Egyptian deity Set, including the Greek version, Seth[21]. (In this essay, I'll call the god – as opposed to the **Doctor Who** character – 'Set', though some of the sources I quote will call him 'Seth'.) Set is probably now best known from the story of Isis and Osiris written by Plutarch, a Greek scholar, in the first century CE[22]. In his version of the tale, the would-be king Set tricks and drowns his brother Osiris, divides the body into pieces, and scatters them all over Egypt[23]. When the goddesses Isis and Nephthys reassemble Osiris's body, he becomes the first mummy. Horus eventually defeats Set and becomes the pharaoh on earth, while Osiris reigns in the afterlife[24]; Set is tried for his crimes and punished, though not with death. Plutarch's story is supplemented by a New Kingdom Egyptian papyrus, *The Contendings of Horus and Seth*, the comical story of Horus and Set's fight before the court of the gods over who should become king.

However, these are later versions of the tale: Horus and Set were two of Egypt's oldest deities, and the story of their conflict was one

---

[21] Te Velde, Herman, *Seth: God of Confusion*, p1.

[22] Plutarch, *Moralia*, trans Frank C Babbitt.

[23] Set's attempt to ensure Osiris' permanent demise is not dissimilar to the Time Lord's destruction of the body of Morbius as described in *The Brain of Morbius* episode 2 (1976): 'His body was placed in a dispersal chamber and atomised to the nine corners of the universe.' I wonder if Robert Holmes recalled this detail from Egyptian mythology when he was reworking Terrance Dicks' script.

[24] Pinch, Geraldine, *Egyptian Mythology*, p78.

of its oldest myths[25] – congruent with the basis of *Pyramids of Mars*, in which the Osirans' contact with Ancient Egypt dates to the time of the country's founding. The story is recorded in the Pyramid Texts engraved in the tombs of pharaohs of the Old Kingdom – although not as a neat narrative like Plutarch's account, but in references and allusions. Priests and kings would have understood those mentions, in something like the way I can talk about **Doctor Who** in this essay without having to explain the basics of the show to the reader.

In their fight, Set destroys one of Horus's eyes, and Horus destroys Set's testicles. The eyes of Horus, the falcon god of the sky, were thought of as the moon (the left eye, harmed by Set) and the sun[26]. (Sarah calls Horus 'god of light'[27]. Perhaps she is only being metaphorical; or perhaps she has this connection in mind.) As well as crediting the pharaoh with restoring Horus's eye, the Pyramid Texts also describe the gods' expedition, led by the moon-god Thoth, to retrieve the eye from Set – who is said to have trampled on it and eaten it. (If these details seem contradictory, it's because they are. I'll return to the internal inconsistences of Egyptian mythology later.)

The Eye of Horus appears throughout Egyptian art and mythology (Set's testicles are mentioned rather less often) and plays an important role in *Pyramids*. It was one of the most popular amulets, and a symbol used to protect both the living and the dead: depicted as a human eye with the markings that surround the eye

---

[25] Griffiths, J Gwyn, *The Conflict of Horus and Seth from Egyptian and Classical Sources*, pp1-4.
[26] Mercer, Samuel AB, *Horus: Royal God of Egypt*, pp150-51.
[27] Episode 1.

of a falcon[28], it was painted on coffins, in tombs, and on the prows of boats, and placed over the incision made on mummies to remove the internal organs for embalming[29]. The Eye of Horus functions in *Pyramids* much as it did in Ancient Egypt: as the embodiment of Horus's protecting power[30].

In *Pyramids* Sutekh's eyes, too, have power – in fact, his mask is marked with two Eyes of Horus, as if again to warn or to contain his deadly mental force. Glowing eyes are one of the few elements to survive from Lewis Greifer's original outline, along with the return of an evil alien-god and a rocket launch which must be stopped[31].

The Egyptians loved plays on words, and this is one: 'eye' in Ancient Egyptian is 'irt', and the verb 'iri', 'to do, to act, to create' can be written with just the eye hieroglyph[32]. A god's eye is the personification of their power[33]. Rivka B Kern Ulmer writes: 'the

---

[28] Ulmer, Rivka B Kern, 'The Divine Eye in Ancient Egypt and in the Midrashic Interpretation of Formative Judaism'. *Journal of Religion and Society* #5, 2003, p274.

[29] Wilkinson, Richard H, *Reading Egyptian Art: A Hieroglyphic Guide to Ancient Egyptian Painting and Sculpture*, p43.

[30] The script, bathetically, describes the Eye of Horus on Mars as 'a red crystal rugby football' pulsating 'like a pedestrian crossing beacon'. (Wiggins, Martin, 'Infotext', *Pyramids of Mars* DVD.) There is just enough resemblance between the round red oval of the televised Eye on its white lotus, and a painted carving of King Tut's egg-shaped, copper-red head emerging from a white-and-pale-blue lotus, to make me wonder if the designers might have been influenced by pictures of it.

[31] Pixley, 'Archive', p33.

[32] Faulkner, Raymond O, *A Concise Dictionary of Middle Egyptian*, pp25-27.

[33] Pinch, *Egyptian Mythology*, p128.

eye is the chief organ by which visual power is transmitted, notwithstanding if the eye belongs to a god, a human being, or a natural phenomenon, such as the sun.'[34] In *Pyramids*, the Eye of Horus is a literal transmitter of Horus's power (or perhaps the combined might of his hundreds of allies). We don't know what kind of power it uses to keep Sutekh paralysed in his tomb: it might be a radio signal like the warning sent to Earth, or a psychic force, or some other, unknown energy. The only thing we can be sure of is that, like all matter and energy in the universe, it can't travel faster than the speed of light – so this, at least, is not 'contrary to the laws of the universe'[35]. In fact, by holding back Sutekh's destructiveness, it is maintaining the order of the cosmos.

'The Servant of Sutekh'

The Doctor tells us that '[t]he whole of Egyptian culture is founded upon the Osiran pattern.'[36] For the Ancient Egyptians, the dead king (and, eventually, every deceased person) was identified with the god Osiris, and the living king with his son and avenger, Horus. Perhaps the Egyptians of the **Doctor Who** universe would have absorbed this concept from their alien visitors: a replaying of the real events of the Osiran conflict and Horus's victory. Another key Egyptian concept might have originated with the Osirans: 'maat', a

---

[34] Ulmer, 'The Divine Eye', p4.
[35] Episode 1. In Episode 4, Sutekh communicates with Marcus Scarman on Mars in real time. Perhaps, in certain circumstances, his 'cytronic control' is capable of 'spooky action at a distance' — Einstein's description of quantum entanglement, in which particles seem to communicate instantly, no matter how far apart they are. We can only guess at the powers of a cytronic particle accelerator. Or perhaps Sutekh is, in fact, violating the laws of space and time?
[36] Episode 2.

word which can be translated as 'truth, justice, righteousness, order, balance, and cosmic law'[37], describing 'the ordering and governing principle of the created world.'[38] This contrasted with 'isfet', 'injustice or wrong, disorder, and unreasonableness'[39].

'The ideal Egyptian gentleman,' writes Herman te Velde, 'is the "ger ma'a", the truly modest, literally the silent man, characterised by self-control [...] He lives in accordance with maat.'[40] By contrast, a papyrus describes the 'follower of Seth' – not a cultist, but 'a potentially violent, decadent, and debauched man and a womaniser' who drinks to excess. His 'tastes and manners are unrefined, unrestrained and earthy [...] His solitary nature places him as a misfit outside the norms of ideal Egyptian society.'[41] The Sethian man 'disturbs the harmony of ordered existence by his foolish speech and unruly conduct'; like Set himself, he may be branded "shed-kheru", 'which means literally "to raise the voice" and more generally: "to behave incorrectly", "to make mischief", "to stir up strife", "to kick up a row", "to cause commotion".'[42]

Set really was called 'the Destroyer'[43]. However, as befits a god of disorder, Set is not just a cosmic villain, but also a benevolent deity: a benefactor of the pharaoh, and a protector of the sun-god. In the

---

[37] Pinch, *Egyptian Mythology*, p159.
[38] Pinch, *Egyptian Mythology*, p65.
[39] Hornung, Erik, *Idea into Image: Essays on Ancient Egyptian Thought*, p136.
[40] Te Velde, Herman, 'The Egyptian God Seth as a Trickster'. *Journal of the American Research Center in Egypt* (JARCE) #7, 1968, p37.
[41] Szpakowska, *Behind Closed Eyes*, pp73-4.
[42] Te Velde, 'Seth as a Trickster', p38.
[43] Leitz, Christian, *Lexikon der Ägyptischen Götter und Götterbezeichnungen*, p669.

Pyramid Texts, Set teams up with Horus to help the spirit of the deceased king. Set and Horus are sometimes shown together crowning the pharaoh, or purifying him or her with jars of water (when Set is out of fashion, Thoth takes his place in these scenes). Horus and Set could even be combined into a two-headed god[44].

In the version of the story given in the Shabako Stone[45], the god Geb first awards Upper Egypt to Set and Lower Egypt to Horus; Egypt can be referred to as 'the portions of the Two Lords, Horus and Seth'. Some scholars argue that stories like this one have their roots in the original unification of Egypt, with war between the two lands eventually peacefully concluded with one king ruling both Lower and Upper Egypt, wearing the 'double crown' which represented both – a pharaoh who incorporated the powers of both Horus and Set and was helped by both gods[46]. Set and Horus are sometimes depicted symbolically 'tying together' the two lands[47]. But in the end, Geb changes his decision and awards the whole of Egypt to Horus, while Set is expelled to the desert.

Maat, the order of society and the universe, 'must be established and actively realised time and again'[48] through correct speech and action, especially by the king. But in fact, pharaoh is described as being **both** Horus and Set: 'Thou goest, Horus goes. Thou speakest,

---

[44] Te Velde, *Seth*, p69.
[45] This pharaoh's name is also transliterated as Shabaka and Shabaqo. The stone, which dates from his reign, is currently in the British Museum.
[46] Griffiths, *The Conflict of Horus and Seth*, pp73-4, 119.
[47] For example, on the throne of Senwosret I. Te Velde, *Seth*, pv.
[48] Hornung, *Idea into Image*, p135.

Seth speaks.'[49] Egyptian kings had an elaborate set of five official titles, including their Horus Name, written with the Horus falcon. However, the Second Dynasty king, Peribsen, had a Set Name instead; and another Second Dynasty pharaoh, Khasekhemui, had both a Horus Name and a Set Name[50]. Much later, during the New Kingdom, Set would be the patron god of many pharaohs, some of whom would name themselves after him: Seti, Setnakhte. Samuel Mercer writes:

> 'Ruling, the king is Horus, when he must use force he is Seth. Neither of the two aspects can be dispensed with. It is the cooperation of the two gods in the king which guarantees the welfare of the world.'[51]

At times, Set was not a threatening figure, but a comic one. In a notoriously rude episode in *The Contendings of Horus and Seth*[52], he attempts to have sex with Horus, who catches his uncle's semen in his hands before it can enter his body. His mother Isis retaliates by placing some of Horus's semen on the lettuce in Set's garden. When Set boasts to the gods that he has shamed his nephew by 'perform[ing] the labour of a male against him', Horus demonstrates with Thoth's help that Set is the one who's been impregnated by 'divine seed' – a 'pregnancy' that produces the

---

[49] Pyramid Texts, Utterance 437, §798a in Griffiths, *The Conflict of Horus and Seth,* p2.
[50] Mercer, *Horus*, p68.
[51] Te Velde, *Seth*, p71.
[52] Simpson, William Kelly, *The Literature of Ancient Egypt*, p121. Another version of the tale gives Set this timeless come-on: 'How beautiful are thy buttocks!' (Dynes, Wayne R, and Stephen Donaldson, eds, *Homosexuality in the Ancient World*, p285.)

moon. Later, in a race between 'stone ships' – ships for transporting stone – Set misunderstands and actually makes his ship out of stone, by cutting off the top of a mountain; not surprisingly, it sinks[53]. Sutekh is anything but funny, but Set's troublemaking nature means he is sometimes ridiculous.

'Adhere to maat,' advises a proverb, 'but do not exaggerate.'[54] A little chaos is a necessary ingredient in the order of things.

'Never Underestimate Sutekh'

When Sarah asks the Doctor why the Osirans didn't kill Sutekh, he explains: 'It's against their code. To have killed him would have meant that they were no better than he, so they simply imprisoned him.'[55] This suggests the Osirans had their own version of maat to follow. But was this the real reason?

In Plutarch's version of the battle between Horus and Set, Isis releases her defeated brother rather than execute him, to her son's chagrin. Were the Osirans motivated by mercy? For an alien with thousands of years to live, being essentially buried alive is a cruel fate. Sutekh's paralysis and entombment is the exact opposite of the happy ending that mummification and burial represented to the Ancient Egyptians. With their bodies safely preserved, and all the necessities of life securely sealed up with them – food, toiletries, clothing, furniture, even servants in the form of 'ushabti' figurines – they could look forward to the comfortable afterlife portrayed in the scenes of parties and relaxation painted on the

---

[53] Simpson, William Kelly, *The Literature of Ancient Egypt*, p122.
[54] 'The Maxims of Ptahhotep', quoted in Hornung, *Idea into Image*, p136.
[55] Episode 2.

walls of their tombs. The spells in the collection called *The Book of Coming Forth by Day* (better known as 'The Book of the Dead') enabled the deceased's spirit to come out of the tomb to visit the living[56]. Perhaps the screen we see in his tomb was provided so that Sutekh could at least observe the world outside his prison.

If their motivation was not mercy, then perhaps the Osirans didn't kill Sutekh because they **couldn't**. Perhaps he was so absurdly powerful that the best they could manage was to leave him '[t]rapped beneath a pyramid and powerless to move'[57] and wait for him to die. Unfortunately for this plan, and for Earth and the rest of the universe, Sutekh outlives the Osirans; by 1911, their 'time [...] is long past'[58]. (Perhaps Sutekh's destruction of their homeworld, Phaester Osiris, was the beginning of their end.) Apparently they did foresee this possibility, setting up the alarm that would radio a readily deciphered warning to whoever was on Earth if Sutekh's prison was opened[59].

---

[56] Kemp, Barry, *How to Read the Egyptian Book of the Dead*, pp47-48.
[57] Episode 2.
[58] Episode 4.
[59] The Doctor's comment about 'e' being the most common letter suggests the message is in English – not impossible, if the Pyramid of Mars has been monitoring Earth – and that the signal uses a simple substitution cipher in which patterns represent each letter, like Morse Code. However, it would be impossible to decipher a phrase as short as 'Beware Sutekh' without the cipher's key. It may be that the Doctor sees '_E___E ___E__' and makes an educated guess that it doesn't say, for example, BECOME FRIEND. It's more like the broadcast includes the key – so the full message is something like 'ABCDEFGHIJKLMNOPQRSTUVWXYZ BEWARE SUTEKH' – or that it contains some other clue to its decipherment.

They also left a warning to anyone who might try to open the door to Sutekh's chamber. In planning for events thousands of years in the future, the Osirans faced a similar problem to one humanity is struggling with: how to warn distant generations about nuclear waste, which will be dangerous for tens of thousands of years. Writing about 'nuclear semiotics' for Forbes Online[60], James Conca remarks, 'King Tut got it really wrong – both tomb raiders and archaeologists didn't believe his warnings of death.' Though in fact Tutankhamun's tomb bore no 'warning of death', the comparison is still very relevant for us. Although the hieroglyphs we see on screen are gibberish, we can assume they represent a written warning left by the Osirans – one which would still have been intelligible until the end of Egyptian history, 3,000 years later (and probably to Marcus Scarman). But most Egyptians (probably including the average tomb robber) could not read, and the Osirans could not have been sure if Egyptian civilisation would last as long as Sutekh would. The burning red stare of the Eye of Horus adds an additional, non-verbal warning. Scarman's workers recognise this warning, especially its preternatural content: there is something extraordinary here, something not of human manufacture. Like any archaeologist in a mummy movie, of course, Marcus Scarman simply ignores the warning[61]. The Osirans' precautions are better on Mars, where they've used 'hostile architecture' – one of the

---

[60] Conca, James, 'Talking to the Future – Hey, There's Nuclear Waste Buried Here!'.

[61] In fact, it's absurdly easy for him to enter the chamber: he merely pokes at the stone slabs making up the door with a small pick, and it obligingly slides open for him.

methods suggested for keeping future humans away from nuclear waste deposits[62].

'The Might of Sutekh'

Another possibility exists for why the Osirans left Sutekh alive: they might have needed him. As I've noted, the mythological god Set is not 'totally evil'[63] but ambiguous: sometimes disruptive, sometimes beneficent. Set had his own temples and priests and was worshipped like any god[64]. His reputation varied over the 3,000 years or so of Ancient Egyptian history: at times Set was the patron god of royalty, at others a hated adversary who was ritually execrated. In different places, too, Set's status could be different; even as his image and name were being chiselled out in the Nile Valley in later times, in the desert oases to the west, he was worshipped until the end. As Eugene Cruz-Uribe puts it, 'he was an integral part of Egyptian culture'[65].

One reason for this is that the Egyptian gods, and the cosmos they had created and maintained, had a far greater enemy than Set: the giant serpent Apep or Apophis, who every night attacked the sun god's boat. Each night, the gods were obliged to repel Apep, or the

---

[62] Perhaps the electrified outer doors in *The Tomb of the Cybermen* are another example of 'hostile architecture' – unless this was the first and simplest of the Cybermen's intelligence tests?

[63] Sarah, episode 2.

[64] Surely I should mention somewhere in this essay my own **Doctor Who** novel *Set Piece* (1995), which is partly set in Ancient Egypt during the reign of Akhenaten, and features an attempted rebellion against that pharaoh's religious reforms by Set's priesthood.

[65] Cruz-Uribe, Eugene, 'Stḫ ꜣ pḥty: "Seth, God of Power and Might"', JARCE #45, 2009, p204.

sun would never rise and the world would collapse back into the chaos from which it had arisen[66].

There are multiple examples of Set depicted spearing Apep, including a papyrus[67] in which the god, known for his strength, stands at the prow of the solar boat and thrusts his lance into the serpent. A passage in the Coffin Texts, which would later became part of the Book of the Dead, describes Apep's hypnotic gaze: 'Now when it is the time of the evening, he will turn his eye towards [the sun god] Re. A standstill comes about among the crew and a great bewilderment during the course.' Set defies Apep: 'You who see from afar, just close your eye!' Many gods and demons had powerful, dangerous eyes: JF Borghouts suggests that Set can beat Apophis in their staring contest over the sun-god's barque because Set has his own 'evil eye'[68].

Imagine, then, that there are even greater threats to the universe than Sutekh – and that the Osirans calculated that, one day, they might need his immense power to pit against an even worse evil.

'Plaything of Sutekh'

By protecting the sun in its nightly journey, Set kept the cycle of time going forwards as it should. Sutekh, by contrast, threatens to end time by reducing everything to chaos, including 'the laws of the

---

[66] Compare the threat if the Doctor doesn't give the assembled Key to Time to the White Guardian 'before the Universe is plunged into eternal chaos'. (*The Ribos Operation* (1978)).
[67] 'A Vignette from the Book of the Dead of Lady Cheritwebeshet'. Getty Images.
[68] Borghouts JF, 'The Evil Eye of Apophis'. *Journal of Egyptian Archaeology* #59, 1973, p115.

universe'[69] and the established future. The task of a pharaoh was to uphold maat[70]; as a Time Lord, the Doctor is the one who must keep history moving correctly. As he tells Laurence: 'Something's interfering with time, Mr Scarman, and time is my business.'[71] Kim Newman points out this exchange in *City of Death* (1979)[72]:

DOCTOR

I can't let you fool about with time.

COUNT SCARLIONI

What else do you ever do?

DOCTOR

Ah, well, I'm a professional.

Newman goes on to say that 'When the Doctor interacts with' antagonists such as Solon and Harrison Chase[73], 'his carefree, amused, interested attitude points up the absurdity of the lunatic villain roles they are so intent on playing.'[74] Unusually, at no time does the Doctor take this approach in *Pyramids*; he is deadly serious from the first, morose scene. This is the Doctor at his most 'professional', signalling the audience that we, too, should believe in Sutekh's threat.

---

[69] Episode 1.

[70] Pinch, *Egyptian Mythology*, p4.

[71] Episode 1.

[72] Newman, Kim, *BFI TV Classics: Doctor Who*, p27.

[73] In *The Brain of Morbius* and *The Seeds of Doom* (1976) respectively.

[74] Newman, *BFI TV Classics: Doctor Who*, p89.

Paradoxically, while the Doctor's task is to preserve order, he himself is a persistent sower of chaos. He has little or no patience for authority or bureaucracy, is always at the centre of conflict, and routinely brings down rulers and governments. Like the shed-kheru, he behaves incorrectly, makes mischief, stirs up strife, kicks up a row, and causes commotion. He is a perpetual outsider, without home or family, as unsettled as he is unsettling. He is, in a word, Sethian.

The Doctor and the god Set both have a lot in common with the mythological archetype called the Trickster, whose restlessness, lack of respect for boundaries and rules, deceit, cunning, and sometimes foolishness cause endless trouble but are also essential to creating and maintaining the order of the world[75].

'Brother to Sutekh'

David Rafer suggests that the 'cosmic struggle' between Horus and Sutekh 'is played out in the earthly conflict between Laurence and

---

[75] The term 'Trickster' is sometimes used in a very loose way to encompass any god or hero who deceives, blurring important differences between cultures. However, the Doctor and Set both share the role some Tricksters have in shaping the cosmos. To give one example, in the Navajo Creation myths, Coyote plays an extensive role – he scatters the stars in the sky and brings death into the world amongst many other disorderly but creative acts. He is 'a rude, interfering and restless individual, who is nonetheless vital to the process of ordered creation'. (Cooper, 'Coyote in Navajo Religion and Cosmology'. *The Canadian Journal of Native Studies* VII 2, 1987, p183.)

Marcus Scarman'[76]. Stories of brother against brother crop up in both Egyptian mythology ('The Tale of the Two Brothers'[77]) and in the mummy movies (*The Curse of the Mummy's Tomb* (1964)). But poor Laurence Scarman is no Horus. While Scarman has the might of Sutekh behind him, Laurence is a mere human being, neither the rightful heir to the power of the Osirans nor a heroic prince; he is more like Plutarch's sentimental Isis who can't bring herself to put her brother to death. Far from being Sutekh/Marcus' staunch opponent, he does everything he can to save his brother, even interfering with the Doctor's efforts against Sutekh. Despite the Doctor's angry insistence that Marcus is 'an animated human cadaver', Laurence is not completely misguided; he knows that without Marcus, Sutekh will once again be powerless. Presumably he hopes that he can snap Marcus out of Sutekh's 'mesmeric influence', both saving his brother and defeating the Osiran. It's a brave and compassionate plan and it costs him his life.

While Sutekh enjoys killing, the Doctor simply doesn't have time or energy to mourn one more casualty in this fight for the survival of Earth and the universe. But the destruction of the entire cosmos is an abstract idea that it's difficult to get excited about. Sarah's grief for Laurence and her anger at the seemingly indifferent Doctor allows us to see the threat at its largest and smallest scales. 'A man has just been murdered!' she cries, but the Doctor corrects her: five

---

[76] Rafer, David, 'Mythic Identity in **Doctor Who**'. Butler, David, ed, *Time and Relative Dissertations in Space: Critical perspectives on Doctor Who*, p131.

[77] An unpleasantly sexist tale of treacherous women. In one version, the brothers are named Anubis and Set. Simpson, *The Literature of Ancient Egypt*, p92.

men have been murdered so far, counting Marcus Scarman, and 'they're merely the first of millions unless Sutekh is stopped.'[78]

This contrast is also played out in the sequence where the Doctor shows Sarah what will happen if they don't stop Sutekh, jumping forward several decades. The sight of an Earth scoured of life is not as affecting as Sarah's tiny '**I'm** from 1980'[79]. The end of the world is no longer abstract: we are looking at the wreckage of Sarah's and the viewers' familiar world of 'pussy cats, fish and chips, and the Liverpool Docks'[80]. The Doctor's perspective encompasses all time and all space; Sarah puts the conflict into human terms for us.

In the end, however, the Doctor fails to stop Sutekh's release. It's time itself – the two minutes' grace period between the destruction of the Eye of Horus and the release of Sutekh – that saves the day[81].

'Sutekh's Gift of Death'

Trapped in the time tunnel, Sutekh threatens to 'destroy the cosmos'[82]. For an Ancient Egyptian magician, this would have been a standard threat, to a demon or even a god: if my patient isn't cured, I'll 'destroy the present order of the world'[83]. The magician

---

[78] Episode 3. In fact, it's six men. It seems more likely the Doctor has miscounted than that, for example, he is deliberately omitting Namin.
[79] Episode 2.
[80] *Planet of the Spiders* (1974) episode 2.
[81] The Doctor had more time than he thought: the closest Mars came to Earth in 1911 was more than four light minutes. Sheehan, William, 'Appendix 1: Oppositions of Mars, 1901-2035'.
[82] *Pyramids of Mars* episode 4.
[83] Shafer, Byron Esel, ed, *Religion in Ancient Egypt: Gods, Myths, and Personal Practice*, p168.

was bluffing; Sutekh isn't. Many of the stories Robert Holmes wrote or script-edited feature 'lurking megalomaniacs'[84] and would-be cosmic tyrants – Morbius, Eldrad, Magnus Greel[85] – but none are in the Osiran's class, except perhaps Davros, who'd like to have the power to destroy all life – 'power that would set [him] up above the gods'[86] – a power Sutekh already possesses. Even the Master never plots universal genocide – not intentionally, anyway. The exact extent of the destruction the Osiran really could wreak isn't clear – could he annihilate a star? A galaxy? – but he is clearly capable of rendering entire planets incapable of supporting life. Davros wants the universe exclusively for his Daleks, but Sutekh wants it for himself, at least according to the Doctor: 'Because you fear that other intelligent lifeforms may grow to rival you in power, so you kill all life wherever you find it.'[87]

'Even faced with a fiend like Sutekh,' writes Andy Murray, the Doctor 'fights words with words and argues the case for his beliefs.'[88] But in the face of Sutekh's implacable devotion to killing, the Doctor is reduced to cursing him – something unique in the series' long history.

---

[84] Murray, Andy, 'The Talons of Robert Holmes'. Butler, *Time and Relative Dissertations in Space*, p218.

[85] In *The Brain of Morbius*, *The Hand of Fear* (1976) and *The Talons of Weng-Chiang*.

[86] *Genesis of the Daleks* (1975). Perhaps inspired by the Doctor's challenge – would he release a microbe that would kill all life? – Davros eventually develops the reality bomb, which will disintegrate all matter in every universe, except for himself and his Daleks (*The Stolen Earth / Journey's End*, 2008). Would even Sutekh go this far?

[87] Episode 4.

[88] Murray, 'The Talons of Robert Holmes', p226.

'The Face of Sutekh'

It's surprising that Ancient Egypt and its rich and colourful history and mythology haven't made more of an appearance in **Doctor Who**[89]. In 53 years there have only been a pair of brief visits to the pyramids[90], an appearance by Queen Nefertiti[91], two more riffs on the mummy movies in *The Daleks' Master Plan* (1965-66) and *Mummy on the Orient Express* (2014), and a handful of other minor references, such as Scaroth the Jagaroth's appearance as a god in a papyrus scroll[92] and the Doctor's misidentification of Osiris-Re from the tomb of Queen Nefertari as 'Khnum'[93].

---

[89] We have only the title of a story by Brian Hayles rejected in 1966, 'The Hands of Aten'. (Pixley, Andrew, 'Archive: The Celestial Toymaker'. DWM #196, p26.) It may be a reference to a very common image from the time of Akhenaten, the pharaoh who forbade the worship of all gods except the Aten, the sun-disc. The sun's rays were represented as long arms ending in hands that offered Akhenaten and his family the 'ankh', the hieroglyph that means 'life'. Whether this indicates the story was set in Ancient Egypt or drew on Egyptian mythology we may never know.

[90] *The Daleks' Master Plan* (1965-6) and *The Wedding of River Song* (2011).

[91] *Dinosaurs on a Spaceship* (2012).

[92] *City of Death* (1979).

[93] *The Dæmons* episode 3 (1971). The Doctor's speech and slides are evidently derived from the entry 'Horns' in the partwork magazine *Man, Myth, and Magic* (Cavendish, Richard, ed), which identifies the figure as 'the sun god shown with Khnum's head'. The confusion is understandable; many Egyptian gods could be represented with the head of a ram. The figure the Doctor identifies as 'a Hindu demon' appears in the same article; it also appears in the section on Islam in the chapter on Persian mythology in the original 1959 version of the *Larousse Encyclopedia*

Perhaps it's only been a problem of budget: on the big screen, Egypt requires at least some effort at spectacle, even if only on a soundstage. Bringing Egypt to England introduces an outside threat into a less expensive setting – and a more familiar one. A visit to Egypt, even a simulated one, would not only be costly, it would make the companion (and the viewer) an outsider, obliged to try to understand and fit into an 'alien' world[94].

Robert Holmes' source for Egyptian myth was the *New Larousse Encyclopedia of Mythology*[95]. To give the reader an idea of the vast number of gods worshipped in Ancient Egypt, the Encyclopedia remarks: 'a list found in the tomb of Thutmosis III enumerates no fewer than seven hundred and forty.'[96] This is surely Robert Holmes' source for the number of Osirans whose combined might was required to defeat Sutekh (and, presumably, Sarah has read the book!). However, not every god on Thutmosis' long list would

---

of Mythology (Guirand, Felix, ed, p337), where it is identified as 'The black angel [presumably Satan?], depicted with the features of a rackhasa' or rakshasha – a demonic figure from Hindu mythology. Here, the illustration is attributed to 'Treatise on Astrology and Divination' by Mohammed al-Sudi, held at the Bibliothèque Nationale in Paris (the name of which accompanies the image in *Man, Myth, and Magic* – this caption is visible, though not legible, on screen). Now you know.

[94] The setting may be familiar to British viewers, but for an Australian growing up in the 70s, a country estate in Edwardian England or the streets and houses of contemporary London were, in their way, as exotic as Ancient Egypt or Mars.

[95] Pixley, Andrew, 'Pyramids of Mars: Archive Extra'. DWM Special Edition #8, p35.

[96] Guirand, Felix, ed, *New Larousse Encyclopedia of Mythology* (1968), p10.

have had their own temple and priests, as the Encyclopedia implies. Rather, Thutmosis' list is a roll-call of the gods who appear (along with 167 other supernatural entities) in another of the afterlife books, the *Amduat*, or 'What is in the Netherworld', which tells the story of the sun's nightly journey. The *Amduat* appears in many places, but only Thutmosis III has a catalogue with the images and names of all the gods – a catalogue which, interestingly, includes Set, who joins with the goddesses Isis and Selket to defeat Apophis[97].

Why weren't any of the hundreds of other Osirans equal in power to Sutekh? The Doctor tells us the Osirans had 'dome-shaped heads and cerebrums like spiral staircases'[98], but that doesn't describe Sutekh (or any Egyptian god I can think of). Barry Letts suggested the Osirans might not be a single species, but a galactic federation of multiple alien peoples whose many different features inspired the Ancient Egyptians to imagine their gods with the heads of animals, such as falcons, jackals, and lionesses[99].

It's worth mentioning that this was just a way of depicting divinity, symbolically associating the gods with the superhuman powers of animals; a deity could be painted or sculpted as human, part-human and part-animal, or in fully animal form. Intriguingly, though there are plenty of theories, no-one has been able to positively

---

[97] Hornung, Erik, *The Ancient Egyptian Books of the Afterlife*, p33, 38.
[98] Episode 4.
[99] Pixley, 'Archive'. In this case, presumably there was an entire species of square-eared 'Typhonians' at one time. Were they just as powerful as Sutekh? Presumably not, or it wouldn't have taken so many Osirans to stop him. Was he the last of his people? Had he killed all the others – potential rivals to his power?

identify which animal Set's head belongs to; nothing in nature has those long, square ears. The Doctor remarks that the Greeks called Sutekh 'the Typhonian beast'[100], but that phrase actually refers to this creature, also called the 'Set-animal'. The Ancient Greeks identified Set with Typhon, a monster from their own mythology. It would make sense if the animal that represented the god of disorder was a completely mythological one – or a completely alien one, with no Earthly analogue.

Multiple Holmes villains keep their hideous face hidden until a startling reveal – faces either maimed (Greel, Sharaz Jek[101]) or alien (Linx[102] and Sutekh)[103]. We glimpse Sutekh's malevolent, unnatural face in the story's opening, but its displacement of the head of Marcus Scarman, as he channels Sutekh's power to destroy the Eye of Horus, is one of the story's most effectively frightening moments.

'Trapped beneath a pyramid and powerless to move'

Set appears in Lewis Greifer's original outline for *Pyramids of Mars*, but there the chief villain is Set's agent, Sebek, whose crocodile-headed mummy comes alive at the British Museum. It's not immediately clear why the writer chose Sebek, aka Sobek, who

---

[100] Episode 4. I'm not sure where Robert Holmes found this particular phrase – the *New Larousse Encyclopedia of Mythology* (1968) refers to the 'Typhonian animal' (p20). Other animals linked to Set, such as the donkey and hippopotamus, can also be called 'Typhonian beasts' or 'Sethian animals'.

[101] In *The Talons of Weng-Chiang* and *The Caves of Androzani* (1984).

[102] In *The Time Warrior* (1973-74).

[103] The eponymous Brain of Morbius is the ultimate faceless horror.

didn't share Set's bad reputation. The two gods aren't closely connected in mythology or theology; while Set ruled the deserts and foreign lands, Sobek was Lord of the Nile, Lord of the Marsh[104], and Lord of Water[105]. However, they do have the crocodile in common. The animal that was a symbol of divine power for Sobek's worshippers was also execrated as the messenger of Set, or the son of Set[106]. One priest cast aspersions on a temple of Sobek by referring to him as 'Set who has changed into a crocodile'[107]. In the temple of Edfu, Horus is shown spearing Set in the form of crocodile and hippopotamus – powerful and unpredictable animals that were ever-present dangers of the Nile.

For the Egyptians, for whom hieroglyphs were 'the words of the gods', writing the name of a hostile being could be magically dangerous[108]. Each word was spelled out phonetically, then finished off with a 'determinative' hieroglyph to clarify its meaning. Set's name is written with a determinative of the Set-animal – its power neutralised by showing it stabbed with a knife or spear, or tied up. Set's threat can be contained by binding him so that he can't move or act – much as the Osirans left Sutekh paralysed.

---

[104] Pinch, *Egyptian Mythology*, p201.

[105] Spell 285. Faulkner, Raymond O, *The Ancient Egyptian Coffin Texts*, p213.

[106] Te Velde, *Seth*, p150.

[107] Te Velde, *Seth*, p147.

[108] Wilkinson, Richard H, *Symbol and Magic in Egyptian Art*, pp149-51.

Figure 2: *Egyptian hieroglyphs depicting the god Set. At top, he is shown in the form of a seated man with the head of the Set-animal, brandishing a curved sword. Second: the Set-animal. Third: the Set-animal bound to neutralise the magical danger of writing the chaos-god's name. Fourth: Set in the form of a man with the head of a donkey, safely bound to a stake[109].*

[109] The hieroglyphs in this book are from the Aegyptus font by George Douros.

Of course, Greifer might not have been drawing on these loose connections between Set and Sobek; it's possible the idea of an alien with a monstrous crocodile head simply proved irresistible[110]. In a 1937 short story by Robert Bloch, 'The Secret of Sebek'[111], originally published in *Weird Tales*, occultists disturb the mummy of one of Sebek's priests, only for the god himself to wreak his promised revenge in monstrous person. In Bloch's Lovecraftian tale, the gods of Egypt were '[s]trange hybrids', 'elemental creatures'. The gods of historical Egypt were offered food and drink and other everyday necessities, but that's too quotidian for such a milieu; probably drawing on the description in *The Golden Bough* of a supposed much later human sacrifice to the Nile[112], Bloch has his Egyptian priests toss virgins to the sacred crocodiles. Greifer's outline is rather less sadistic. However, it's not impossible that he drew some inspiration from Bloch's story, which contains all the classic elements of a mummy's curse tale and had been anthologised multiple times.

Sebek was dropped from *Pyramids* in rewrites, leaving Set, now Sutekh, as the sole antagonist. This simplifies the story and gives it a stronger villain. It also avoids the problem of trying to create a

---

[110] The costumes of **Doctor Who**'s reptilian Martians, the Ice Warriors, were originally constructed with faux crocodile skin made for the 1963 movie *Cleopatra*. (Wiggins, Martin, 'Infotext', *The Ice Warriors* DVD, 2013.)

[111] Anthologised in Haining, Peter, *The Mummy: Stories of the Living Corpse*.

[112] 'Tradition runs that the old custom was to deck a young virgin in gay apparel and throw her into the river as a sacrifice to obtain a plentiful inundation.' Frazer, Sir James George, *The Golden Bough: A Study in Magic and Religion*. Online text, p370.

convincing crocodile head for Sebek; it would be a shame to have a crocodile-headed alien and **not** have him use those terrifying teeth. Given the later failure of *Talons*'s giant rats, the work of scaring the viewer was surely better achieved with a terrifying voice issuing from a largely unseen face, leaving the mummies to fill the role of this story's monsters.

'MY VENGEANCE STARTS HERE!'

Exploiting others means being constantly nervous that they might turn the tables and exploit you. This has formed the basis of numerous science fiction stories from robot rebellions to matriarchal dystopias[113], as well as countless tales in which decent white British men (and worse, women) are imperilled by fiends from the mysterious, magical, mesmeric East. These stories of 'reverse colonisation' are intended to demonstrate how much in need the dastardly foreigner is of the civilising white conqueror, but they also reveal the anxiety that Fu Manchu and his exotic science, or the Mummy animated by Egypt's lost wisdom, might take their revenge for the Opium Wars or British occupation. As the god Ra warns the audience in George Bernard Shaw's *Caesar and Cleopatra* (1899), 'war is a wolf that may come to your own door'[114]. This nagging guilt and anxiety is the basis of the fiction franchises which inspired *The Talons of Weng-Chiang* and *Pyramids of Mars* (and, less directly, *The Tomb of the Cybermen*).

While the chinoiserie of *Talons* draws on the single source of **Fu Manchu** fiction and films, *Pyramids of Mars* is the inheritor of a

---

[113] *The Robots of Death* (1977) is **Doctor Who**'s answer to the original science fiction robot uprising, the play *RUR* (Karel Čapek, 1920). The (perhaps mercifully) unmade stories *The Hidden Planet* (commissioned in 1963) and *Prison in Space* (commissioned in 1968) would have featured societies in which men are subjugated by women. (Howe, David J, Mark Stammers and Stephen James Walker, *Doctor Who: The Handbook – The First Doctor*, p238; Bignell, Richard, 'The Missing Stories', DWM #198, p18.)

[114] Quoted in Bulfin, Ailise, 'The Fiction of Gothic Egypt and British Imperial Paranoia: The Curse of the Suez Canal'. *English Literature in Transition, 1880-1920*, 54(4), p432.

longer tradition of 'Egyptomania' which started in the early 19th century with the deciphering of hieroglyphs and the publication of the multi-volume, richly-illustrated, and wildly successful *Description de l'Égypte*[115]. France and Britain, rivals for control of Egypt, shipped home obelisks from the city of Luxor to stand in Paris and London. In Victorian Britain, Egypt was everywhere: at exhibitions, public mummy unwrappings, and the opera (Verdi's *Aida*); in 'Egyptian Revival' architecture and jewellery; in the design of crockery, cigarette cases, and advertising; and in plays, pop songs, and in the popular fiction that is the ancestor of *Pyramids*.

The late-Victorian boom in what Roger Luckhurst calls 'Egyptian Gothic'[116] literature had its roots in unease over the construction of the Suez Canal[117], a joint project between Egypt and Britain's imperial rival, France. The canal, completed in 1869, connected the Mediterranean Sea to the Red Sea and thus Britain to its colonies in India and elsewhere. It became quickly crucial to the Empire – leading the British, anxious at leaving the control of such a resource in foreign hands, to occupy Egypt in 1882. After this time, fiction about Egypt shifted from tales of wonder to nervous stories of untrustworthy natives and supernatural danger[118], brought home with mummies and treasures to the heart of the Empire itself[119].

---

[115] Lupton, Carter, '"Mummymania"' for the Masses': Is Egyptology Cursed by the Mummy's Curse?'. MacDonald, Sally, and Michael Rice, eds, *Consuming Ancient Egypt*, p23.
[116] Luckhurst, Roger, *The Mummy's Curse: The True History of a Dark Fantasy*, p153.
[117] Bulfin, 'The Fiction of Gothic Egypt', p412.
[118] Luckhurst, *The Mummy's Curse*, p209.
[119] Bulfin, 'The Fiction of Gothic Egypt', p413.

'I Saw a Mummy'

Like science fiction itself, mummy stories got their start with a teenage girl. The earliest story of an Egyptian mummy brought back to life is the 1827 science fiction novel *The Mummy – A Tale of the Twenty-Second Century* by Jane Webb (later Jane C Loudon) – 19 years old when she put pen to paper – in which the revived King Kheops critiques a degenerate future society[120]. One of the earliest curse-of-the-mummy tales, *Lost in a Pyramid; or the Mummy's Curse* (1869), is also attributed to a woman, Louisa May Alcott, best known for the previous year's *Little Women*[121].

Some mummy stories were tragic romances, such as Sir Arthur Conan Doyle's *The Ring of Thoth* (1890), which involved an immortal Ancient Egyptian pining for his mummified lover. However, romances were outnumbered two to one by curse stories[122], 'scores' of which appeared after the British occupation of Egypt, persisting into the following decades: Ailise Bulfin has counted more than 100 between 1860 and 1914[123]. Doyle's *Lot No 249* (1892), with its ghastly Egyptian corpse killing at the command of its vengeful owner, brings us closer to the familiar mummy of the movies, and the robotic mummies of *Pyramids*.

Bram Stoker's novel *The Jewel of Seven Stars* (1903) is less well-known than *Dracula* (1897), but has also been highly influential. It

---

[120] Lupton, '"Mummymania" for the Masses', p24.

[121] An earlier story, *The Mummy's Soul* (1862), was published anonymously in an American magazine. *Lost in a Pyramid* was published in both the US and the UK in 1869. (Bulfin, 'The Fiction of Gothic Egypt', p440 nn29 and 30.)

[122] Bulfin, 'The Fiction of Gothic Egypt', p420.

[123] Bulfin, 'The Fiction of Gothic Egypt', p418.

adds the element of reincarnation – alien to the Ancient Egyptians, but familiar to the Victorians from contact with Hindu and Buddhist ideas. The spirit of the evil Queen Tera attempts to possess the archaeologist Abel Trelawny's daughter Margaret. *Jewel* has elements in common with H Rider Haggard's popular *She* (1887): although the only mummies in *She* are used as firewood, the story involves an ancient African civilisation, a royal woman, an immortal pining for their lost love, and reincarnation[124].

We can see echoes of *She* and especially of *The Jewel of Seven Stars* in *The Hand of Fear* (1976), with its ancient, (temporarily) female tyrant and her burial and revival[125]. While Eldrad's hand is all that was left of the Kastrian tyrant, Queen Tera's seven-fingered hand is broken off by a tomb-robber, resulting in a sympathetic scar on the wrist of Margaret Trelawny. Eldrad's hypnotic ring recalls the ring found with Tera's mummy (set with a large ruby carved with an image of the seven stars of the Plough) and also Doyle's Ring of

---

[124] The cover of the 2006 Broadview edition of the novel is a portrait of the 21st Dynasty mummy of Nesi-Khonsu, suggesting Ayesha's immortality, but also her eventual demise as the fire of immortality paradoxically withers her away. It seems probable that this inspired the volcanic flame that can both heal and kill in *The Brain of Morbius* and *Planet of Fire* (1984).

[125] A likely inspiration for the **Doctor Who** show-makers would be Hammer's 1971 adaptation of *Jewel* as *Blood from the Mummy's Tomb*, which prominently features a crawling, disembodied hand. In fact, this seems like a more probable source for *Hand of Fear* than the movie mentioned by Robert Holmes (Russell, 'Interview'), *The Hands of Orlac* (most probably the 1960 version), in which the devilish hands stay firmly attached. (There are a perhaps surprising number of horror movies featuring evil hands on the loose.)

Thoth ('a massive ring with a large crystal set in it'[126]). Ayesha, the eponymous She-who-must-be-obeyed, recognises her reincarnated love thanks to the Ancient Egyptian ring he's wearing. Ibrahim Namin has his own 'magic ring' in *Pyramids*, flashing green as he commands his robotic servants.

These stories expressed – and perhaps fuelled – what Bulfin refers to as 'imperial paranoia'[127]. Even as the Empire continued to expand[128], confidence was wavering in the face of:

> 'The decay of British global influence, the loss of overseas markets for British goods, the economic and political rise of Germany and the United States, the increasing unrest in British colonies and possessions, the growing domestic uneasiness over the morality of imperialism'.

Could Britain keep control of Egypt and the vital Suez Canal? What if another colonial power took it over? What if nationalist uprisings in Egypt and the Sudan succeeded in ousting their British masters? Would it be more dangerous for Britain to remain in Egypt or to withdraw? Were the Britons 'degenerating' as a race (they saw modern Egyptians as the 'degenerate' descendants of the admirable ancients[129]) and might other races – like Dracula, 'more

---

[126] Doyle, Arthur Conan, 'The Ring of Thoth', *The Captain of the Pole Star and Other Tales*, p184.

[127] Bulfin, 'The Fiction of Gothic Egypt', passim.

[128] 'Anxious or not,' points out Nicholas Daly, between 1870 and 1900 the British Empire added over 5,000,000 square miles of new territory (*Modernism, Romance, and the Fin de Siècle*, p32).

[129] Bulfin, 'The Fiction of Gothic Egypt', p426.

vigorous, more fecund'[130] – in turn colonise Britain? Dracula is overcome by Western men, but *The Jewel of Seven Stars* ends with the destruction of its English protagonists by the forces they release – a conclusion so alarming that in subsequent editions it was replaced with a conventional happy ending[131].

Infection, real or metaphorical, is a common theme in tales of reverse colonisation – perhaps not surprising, given the frequency with which Europeans have (sometimes intentionally) decimated populations on other continents with disease. Colonised countries were feared as a source of disease[132], a danger both to Britons who visited those countries and to Britain itself. A literal plague follows the travellers from Egypt back to contemporary London in Guy Boothby's novel *Pharos, the Egyptian* (1899), reversing the Biblical story: 'here Egypt brings plague down on the houses of its implacable enemy.'[133]

Sometimes infection is the start of a change into, if you will, a foreign body. Jonathan Harker is horrified by Dracula's plan to settle in London and 'create a new and ever-widening circle of semi-demons' as the infection of vampirism spreads. Stephen D Arata writes:

---

[130] Arata, Stephen D, 'The Occidental Tourist: *Dracula* and the Anxiety of Reverse Colonization'. *Victorian Studies* 33(4), p640.

[131] As a child, I read an 'abridged' version of *Jewel* which had the original downbeat finale, and was so confused by the goodies' failure to win that for many years I thought 'abridged' meant literally that the ending had been left off.

[132] Bulfin, 'The Fiction of Gothic Egypt', p425.

[133] Luckhurst, *The Mummy's Curse*, p168.

'In *Dracula* vampirism designates a kind of colonisation of the body. Horror arises not because Dracula destroys bodies, but because he appropriates and transforms them. Having yielded to his assault, one literally "goes native" by becoming a vampire oneself.'[134]

Jewel's Margaret Trelawney, who was born while her father was entranced in Tera's tomb, seems to share not just her appearance but a 'dual existence' with the Queen; she changes inexorably into her 'new self'[135] – an Ancient Egyptian.

This infection-followed-by-metamorphosis, this 'colonisation of [...] bodies'[136], has become a commonplace in speculative fiction, not excepting **Doctor Who**. In *The Tomb of the Cybermen*, the Telos expedition penetrate the Cybermen's resting place and revive the cyborgs, preserved like mummies in their giant freezer, only to be told by the Cybercontroller: 'You will become the first of a new race of Cybermen. You will return to the Earth and control it.'[137] The first step is the replacement of Toberman's arms with robotic ones.

The Ark in Space (1975) features another alienated arm. Driven from their home planets by human colonists, the insect-like Wirrn plan to transform the people hibernating in the Ark into more of their own kind; the Ark's leader, Noah, battles his own Wirrn-infected hand for control. In *The Seeds of Doom* (1976), the Krynoid transforms humans into miniature versions of itself. In each case, it starts with an infecting touch to the arm: first the scientist Winlett,

---

134 Arata, 'The Occidental Tourist', p630.
135 Stoker, Bram, *The Jewel of Seven Stars*, p 158.
136 Arata, 'The Occidental Tourist', pp 629-630.
137 *The Tomb of the Cybermen* episode 3.

who escapes before a planned amputation; then very nearly Sarah Jane, her arm held close to the opening Krynoid pod; and finally Keeler. The image of the infecting or infected hand or arm recurs again and again[138]: the colonisation of the mind starts with a colonisation of the body.

By contrast with these **Doctor Who** stories and with *The Jewel of Seven Stars*, Sutekh possesses both mind and body instantly, intangibly, and completely – at a glance.

'If you cross the threshold of the gods, you will die!'[139]

The skin is one boundary; there are also boundaries between peoples and nations, colonisers and colonised. Contact with non-white people meant increasing moral panic over 'contamination' of the white race. This fear expressed itself in fantastical examples such as the 'psycho-hybrid' in Sax Rohmer's Egyptian Gothic novel *The Green Eyes of Bast* (1920). A cat-spirit appears to an Englishwoman in Zagazig, a town near the ancient city of the cat-goddess Bast or Bastet: she gives birth to a daughter with catlike traits. The literal mixing of Eastern and Western blood in *Dracula* is an obvious metaphor for this dread of 'pollution'. On the first page of the novel, Jonathan Harker marks the moment he crosses from West to East, passing over the Danube River in Budapest –

---

[138] Hammer's *The Curse of the Mummy's Tomb* is rather keen on severed hands; Prince Ra-Antef is obliged to strangle his victims one-handed. In the follow-up *The Mummy's Shroud* (1967), Sir Basil Walden is bitten on the arm by a snake the moment he opens the tomb of Prince Kha-To-Bey – perhaps a play on Lord Carnarvon's fatal mosquito bite.
[139] This is what Ahmed cries out when he and the other workers flee the tomb in Episode 1 (Wiggins, 'Infotext', *Pyramids of Mars*).

'traversing a boundary he considers symbolic'[140]. In *Pyramids of Mars*, the moment Marcus Scarman crosses 'the threshold of the gods', he stops being Scarman and starts being a kind of mummy – overwhelmed by a force more ancient and more powerful than either Dracula or Queen Tera.

Scarman returns to England as the embodiment of Sutekh's will, resulting in the deaths of his brother, his friend, his butler, and even a poacher who happens to be on his grounds. Not only do those around him die – 'merely the first of millions unless Sutekh is stopped'[141] – but he himself has been changed into 'a walking mummy': like one of Dracula's victims, he is neither dead nor alive. He has crossed a boundary to return transformed and lethal to his own kind: to Englishmen, to human beings, to all living things.

'Mingle With the Mummies'

The 20th century saw a fresh burst of Egyptomania with the discovery of King Tutankhamun's tomb by archaeologist Howard Carter in 1922. It was one of the richest finds to date: an almost untouched royal tomb, complete with sarcophagus and mummy, and packed with treasures for 'King Tut' to enjoy in his afterlife. Exclusive coverage of the tomb's exploration was given to *The Times*. Stuck for a story, other newspapers turned to the occultists who were circulating rumours of a pharaoh's curse, which were given a tremendous boost when the expedition's financial backer, Lord Carnarvon, fell ill from an infected mosquito bite, finally dying exactly five months after the tomb's steps were found[142]. The fact

---

[140] Arata, 'The Occidental Tourist', p636.
[141] *Pyramids of Mars* episode 3.
[142] Lupton, '"Mummymania" for the Masses', p31.

that Tut's tomb contained no curse[143], and that the actual discoverer, Howard Carter, was left untouched, made no difference. There had been plenty of supposedly haunted mummies before the discovery, but the find – and the curse – were an international sensation.

The popular image of the mummy began with Universal's 1932 classic *The Mummy*, which combined elements of the Tut find with Gothic Egyptian literature. While there had been many silent movies about mummies[144], *The Mummy* was the first talkie, and the first to show one walking around[145] – although Boris Karloff's Imhotep quickly gets out of his wrappings; the familiar mummy shambling around in its bandages wouldn't arrive until Universal's cheap war-time sequels. The first movie sets out the basic premise for all of these films: an Ancient Egyptian priest tries to resurrect his beloved princess. He is punished for this blasphemy by being 'mummified' alive and cursed to guard her tomb for eternity; she is reincarnated in the form of the film's leading lady. The modern-day archaeologists who open the tomb face the mummy's revenge. As Jasmine Day puts it: 'in cinema Carter gets the comeuppance he never received in life.'[146]

---

[143] Silverman, David P, *Ancient Egypt*, p146.

[144] Lupton, '"Mummymania" for the Masses', p36-37.

[145] Day, Jasmine, *The Mummy's Curse: Mummymania in the English-speaking World*, p64.

[146] Day, *The Mummy's Curse*, p75.

Table 1: The Classic Mummy Movies at a Glance

Universal	*The Mummy*	1932
	The Mummy's Hand	1940
	The Mummy's Tomb	1942
	The Mummy's Ghost	1944
	The Mummy's Curse	1944
Hammer	*The Mummy*	1959
	The Curse of the Mummy's Tomb	1964
	The Mummy's Shroud	1967
	Blood from the Mummy's Tomb	1971

The Mummy (1932) was developed from a storyline by Nina Wilcox Putnam and Richard Schayer[147], about an ancient Egyptian wizard who keeps himself alive with injections of a magic potion, and murders women who resemble his long-lost lover. This was apparently written around the same time as Tut's tomb was opened, and so was unlikely to have been influenced by the 'curse'. John Balderston, who had adapted *Dracula* and *Frankenstein* (both 1931) for Universal and was developing a screenplay for *She*, and who as a journalist had covered the discovery of Tutankhamun, is apparently responsible for the elements of the tomb, the curse, the princess (named after Tutankhamun's sister-wife, Ankhesenamun), and the living mummy[148]. The resulting movie is something like a

---

[147] Joshi, ST, *Icons of Horror and the Supernatural*, Volume 1, p395.
[148] Lupton, '"Mummymania" for the Masses', p34.

cross between *The Jewel of Seven Stars* and *Dracula*, with the undead Imhotep hypnotically seducing the half-Egyptian, half-English Helen, promising her eternal life if she will only let him kill her first. In fact, Tom Johnson remarks that *The Mummy* is 'almost a remake' of *Dracula*[149]. The movie was a smash hit, breaking box-office records in the United Kingdom[150]. It was followed by four more films which firmly established the image of the mobile, murderous mummy.

After a 15-year rest, the mummy enjoyed a fresh outing with Hammer's 1959 remake of *The Mummy* and its three sequels, which are the direct basis of *Pyramids*[151]. Robert Holmes remarked, 'I wanted a re-run of *Curse of the Mummy's Tomb* or one of those.'[152] One reason Lewis Greifer's original scripts were set aside was that they underused the trappings of cinema, particularly the Hammer films: 'giant mummies wrapped in decaying bandages stalking their victims through studio fog'[153].

Hammer Film Productions' *The Mummy* was not a direct remake, but more a remix. Scriptwriter Jimmy Sangster remarked: 'I was allowed by Universal, since they were financing the picture, to lift sequences and characters from their earlier movies. This is actually

---

[149] Johnson, Tom, *Censored Screams: The British Ban on Hollywood Horror in the Thirties*, p77.
[150] Johnson, Tom, *Censored Screams*, p84.
[151] For reasons of relevance and space, in this essay I won't discuss Universal's 1999 remake of *The Mummy* and its many sequels and spin-offs.
[152] Russell, 'Interview'.
[153] Robert Holmes, quoted in Pixley, 'Archive'.

more difficult for a writer than coming up with something original.'[154]

Unlike earlier Gothic stories, which were usually set in the past, both *Jewel* and Stoker's more famous novel, *Dracula* (1897), chiefly take place in London in contemporary times; rather like **Doctor Who** placing 'a Yeti on the loo in Tooting Bec', to borrow Jon Pertwee's memorable phrase, Stoker '[brought] the terror of the Gothic home'[155]. What was a here-and-now setting for Stoker has become a period setting for Hammer – and thus for *Pyramids*. *The Mummy* takes place in 1895, and its sequel, *The Curse of the Mummy's Tomb*, in 1900. David Huckvale notes that the designers of these two movies 'went to just as much trouble to recreate the atmosphere of Victorian England as of Ancient Egypt'[156]. This fits with Hammer's other horror movies based on classic (and out of copyright) literature: *The Curse of Frankenstein* (1957), *Dracula* (1958), *The Two Faces of Dr Jekyll* (1960), *The Phantom of the Opera* (1962) and *The Vampire Lovers* (1970, based on Sheridan Le Fanu's *Carmilla*), together with their various sequels. Linking their horror movies with high literature in this way must have helped lend legitimacy to what otherwise might be dismissed as trash. Jasmine Day also suggests an element of 'nostalgia for times when European colonialism held sway'[157] – a time, in fact, when

---

[154] Apparently this problem was not shared by Robert Holmes, who commented, 'When I was script editor I was always "ripping off" the classic horror films and things.' Russell, 'Interview'.

[155] Arata, 'The Occidental Tourist', p621.

[156] Huckvale, David, *Touchstones of Gothic Horror: A Film Genealogy of Eleven Motifs and Images*, p194.

[157] Day, *The Mummy's Curse*, p68.

antiquities were being illegally removed from Egypt in quantity[158]. Surely it's no coincidence that Hammer's *Mummy* made its appearance three years after the Suez Crisis – a failed re-invasion of Egypt seen as the end for the already tottering British Empire[159].

The Mummy's Shroud also has a period setting, this time 1920. Clearly drawing on the 1922 Tut expedition, it concerns the lost tomb of a boy-king, and, like *Curse*, includes the demise of the expedition's financier at the mummy's hands[160]. Hammer's last mummy movie, *Blood from the Mummy's Tomb*, is an adaptation of *The Jewel of Seven Stars*: an anomaly, it's given a contemporary setting and features not a well-wrapped male mummy but a scantily-clad female one. Most of Hammer's mummy movies were shown on TV in the years before the production of *Pyramids*[161].

The spell that animates the mummy is a standard element in the movies, written on a scroll or on the mummy's eponymous Shroud. The Scroll of Thoth, whose spell breathes life back into Imhotep in

---

[158] Magee, Peter, 'The Foundations of Antiquities Departments'. Potts, DT, ed, *A Companion to the Archaeology of the Ancient Near East*, pp72-73.

[159] Bulfin, 'The Fiction of Gothic Egypt', p438.

[160] Well, hand, in the case of *Curse*.

[161] A search of Gale Artemis: Primary Sources, an online database of British publications, found TV listings for *Shroud* in 1971 (with a repeat in early 1975), *Curse* in 1972, and *The Mummy* itself on Boxing Day 1972. I was unable to find any television listings for *Blood from the Mummy's Tomb* before the 1980s. Additionally, the BBC screened the Hammer Horror parody *Carry on Screaming!* (1966), featuring the living mummy of King Rubbatiti, in October 1974 (BBC Genome Project). The ubiquity of mummies in parody reflects the impact of Universal; in fact, *Abbott and Costello Meet the Mummy* (1955) is technically the last Universal mummy movie.

Universal's *The Mummy*, may be derived from a genuine Egyptian tale[162], the story of Setne Khamwas, a magician who seeks a book of powerful magic spells written by the god Thoth himself[163]. The animating spell appears in *Pyramids* as the hocus-pocus which Namin uses to animate his robot mummy servants[164].

In the first of Universal's sequels, *The Mummy's Hand*, the character of Imhotep is split into two: the character type Jasmine Day calls the 'high priest'[165], who is a modern Egyptian, and the silent, bandaged mummy whom he controls. This may have been prompted by practical difficulties with the screen mummies' makeup, which made it difficult or impossible for them to deliver lines[166]. It's similar to the division of labour between articulate villain and less-articulate or inarticulate monster in many **Doctor Who** stories: Solon and the Morbius monster, Li H'Sen Chang and Mr Sin, Davros and the Daleks. Hammer has its high priest in the form of George Pastell (familiar to **Doctor Who** fans as Eric Klieg

---

[162] Lupton, '"Mummymania" for the Masses', p33.

[163] Lichtheim, Miriam, *Ancient Egyptian Literature: Volume III: The Late Period*, p126.

[164] In episode 1 Namin addresses the robot, in words translated by the DVD 'Infotext' as: 'In the name of Sutekh, I command thee – rise!' However, he is not speaking Ancient Egyptian. It's not impossible it's an attempt at Arabic. However, later on, Namin intones 'a gibberish prayer in an unknown language' (Wiggins, 'Infotext', *Pyramids of Mars*), and I think's more likely his order to the robot is in the same tongue. Perhaps it's Osiran?

[165] Day, Jasmine, 'Repeating Death: The High Priest Character in Mummy Horror Films'. Carruthers, ed, *Histories of Egyptology: Interdisciplinary Measures*.

[166] Day, *The Mummy's Curse*, p87.

from *The Tomb of the Cybermen*) as be-fezzed[167] Egyptian Mehemet Bey in *The Mummy*, and Roger Delgado as the tomb's guardian Hasmid in *The Mummy's Shroud*.

Universal's Imhotep is a full-blown character, and Christopher Lee injects personality and emotion into Hammer's Kharis: 'He was not just a monster. We showed the man he once was.'[168] In the sequels made by both studios, alas, the mummy has become a 'faceless automaton [...] a steamroller with no operator'[169]. The robot mummies of *Pyramids* are literal 'faceless automatons'; they will obey anyone who holds the magic ring – even Sarah. We may feel pity as we watch the doomed priest being buried alive, but there's little or none to be felt for the mummy[170], any more than we feel it for the robots – and we pity Marcus Scarman only at the moment of his release and death.

Of all these movies, *Pyramids* most closely resembles Hammer's *The Mummy*: ignoring a warning, an archaeologist opens an untouched tomb (inside which an eerie green light shines) containing an entity who was punished by being buried alive, and is immediately struck down. A modern Egyptian[171], who worships an

---

[167] Technically, an Egyptian would wear a tarboosh, not a fez. The tasselled red felt hat was official dress in the Ottoman Empire, but is now considered old-fashioned. Moneim, Moataz Abdel, 'The Last of Egypt's Tarboush Makers'. *Asharq al-Awsat*, 28 February 2014.

[168] Johnson, Tom, and Mark A Miller, *The Christopher Lee Filmography: All Theatrical Releases*, p88.

[169] Hogan, David J, *Dark Romance: Sexuality in the Horror Film*, p103.

[170] Day, *The Mummy's Curse,* p88.

[171] Typically educated and well-spoken, the 'high priest' cannot be dismissed as a 'superstitious savage'. Namin even delivers his lines

ancient god, transports items from the tomb, including a sarcophagus, to a country house in England. He sends the mummy out into the surrounding woods to commit a series of strangulations. The mummy, untroubled by shotgun blasts, is a killing machine: 'Each of [Christopher Lee's] steps is determined and unstoppable, but slightly awkward, like that of a large, mechanical robot'.[172] There's even an unfortunate poacher.

It's likely the other films also have contributed imagery. In particular, Bey's self-abasement before the mummy of Prince Ra in *The Curse of the Mummy's Tomb* recalls Namin's before 'the servant of Sutekh'[173], although Bey is asking for death (sparing the hero from the curse) and Namin is pleading for his life. The opening shots of stock footage of the pyramids at Giza is also similar to the shots of Saqqara which open *Pyramids*. It's possible that the climax of Universal's *The Mummy's Tomb*, in which the mummy is (apparently) destroyed inside a burning house, inspired the priory's destruction – although an explosion or fire was a typical **Doctor**

---

in RP. In fact, I wonder whether he might have been one of the foreigners who so worried H Rider Haggard: 'there are plenty of Egyptian students in London of the worst and most dangerous order' (quoted in Luckhurst, *The Mummy's Curse*, p198). Hasmid in *The Mummy's Shroud* is an exception to this dignified tradition. Roger Delgado springs from the shadows in extraordinarily bad brownface, waving a dagger and shouting gibberish. He has begun as he means to go on.

[172] Johnson and Miller, *The Christopher Lee Filmography*, p87.
[173] Episode 1.

Who climax, conveniently erasing the evidence of alien incursions[174].

The scene in which Hammer's Kharis is sealed up in his tomb-within-the-tomb, a sort of cupboard barely large enough to contain Christopher Lee, has a parallel in *The Tomb of the Cybermen* episode 1, in which Victoria almost suffocates inside a sarcophagus-like cabinet designed for revitalising Cybermen. Similarly, in *Pyramids*, our heroes are shut up in confined spaces multiple times. First Sarah and Laurence Scarman are obliged to lie together in the coffin-like confines of a trunk to hide from Marcus Scarman and the mummies; shortly afterwards, they and the Doctor squeeze into the alleged priest hole. On Mars, Sarah is trapped inside the decadron crucible[175]; the narrow, deadly cylinder suggests a sarcophagus, placed upright for display (although Sarah seems more mummy-like when she has been cryogenically frozen and placed inside a transparent 'sarcophagus' on Nerva Beacon in *The Ark in Space*.) For that matter, the Doctor himself becomes a mummy twice: first when he and Sarah disguise him as one of the

---

[174] Stargrove was also burned down by **Doctor Who** at the climax of *Image of the Fendahl*. Barnes, 'The Fact of Fiction: Image of the Fendahl'.

[175] The 'Riddle of the Osirans' is a classic logic puzzle which has shown up everywhere from the movie *Labyrinth* (1986) to Terry Pratchett's **Discworld** books. It was suggested by Philip Hinchcliffe, who remembered it from Franz Kafka's 1926 novel *The Castle*. However, the riddle doesn't appear in that book. Curiously, a double-headed god appears in Chapter 17 of the Book of the Dead, who is called: 'Horus with two heads, the one bearing the truth, the other the lie' (or, more precisely, one bears maat and the other isfet). Bleeker, CJ, *Hathor and Thoth: Two Key Figures of the Ancient Egyptian Religion*, p61.

robots by wrapping him in its bandages, next when Sutekh makes the Doctor his puppet, turning him into a walking 'dead man' like Scarman. (Perhaps we could add a third time: when Sutekh releases him, and he apparently becomes a corpse.)

'An Animated Human Cadaver'

In *Pyramids*, the 'high priest' role is first taken by Namin, then by Marcus Scarman, who destroys him and takes his place as controller of the mummies. This streamlines the story and contributes to the plot, motivating Laurence Scarman's misguided attempts to save his brother – the first of which provides the second cliffhanger, as he stops the Doctor from cutting off Sutekh's contact with Scarman.

Is Marcus Scarman really just a walking corpse, or is this something the Doctor hopes to be true – so that Scarman is disposable? Sutekh describes Scarman as his 'puppet', but he is not literally causing that puppet to move and speak: rather, the archaeologist is his devoted servant, addressing him as 'Master'. As Scarman's testing of the possessed Doctor demonstrates, his minions have been 'brainwashed' into worship: 'Venerate his name and obey him in all things.' Dead or not, some spark of Scarman's personality survives – enough for him to dimly recall his brother Laurence, and to cry 'I'm free!', apparently in his own voice, before his body disintegrates[176]. (A shot of a mummy crumbling into bones and/or dust is de rigueur for the movies, from Imhotep in Universal's *The Mummy* to Prem in Hammer's *The Mummy's Shroud*.)

---

[176] Episodes 3, 4.

Perhaps this is how Sutekh destroyed his homeworld, and how he would have gone on to destroy Earth: by turning everyone around him into an army of destructive – or self-destructive – slaves. His telepathic powers are exceptional: he can even read the mind of a Time Lord. 'If you can do that by mental force, Sutekh,' says the Doctor, 'then nothing can be beyond you.' Plus he can apparently directly attack matter with psychokinetic power, as he does the Eye of Horus[177].

'Some Very Plucky Young Girl'

Screen mummies are less like real mummies – neat, dry, and smelling faintly of resin or spices (or at worst musty)[178] – and more like rotting, disintegrating corpses. In Universal's sequels, Lon Chaney Jr's bandages hang raggedly; in Hammer's *The Mummy*, Christopher Lee's bandages are soaked in ooze from a swamp. The robots in *Pyramids* don't have this dirty, messy appearance, which makes sense – they are technology, not flesh (although we do get to see their skeletons). Even Marcus Scarman looks deathly ill rather than actually dead. For a fully gruesome movie mummy, we need to fast-forward to the new series and *Mummy on the Orient Express*, another typically **Doctor Who** fusion of classic horror and science fiction: the period setting is actually the future, and once again the 'mummy' isn't. Since they both draw on the cinema, *Mummy* naturally shares elements with *Pyramids*, including a sarcophagus, an ancient war, and immortality (or extremely extended life) as a curse rather than a blessing. Also worth mentioning is *The Rings of Akhaten* (2013), which includes a

---

[177] Episode 4.
[178] Kmtsesh, 'What's up with Mummies?'

mummy, a pyramid, and an ancient evil (sun-)god coming to life; the title is a play on the name of the pharaoh Akhenaten, and surely Merry, the Queen of Years, takes her name from his daughter, Meritaten.

Immortality is frequently the real curse in mummy stories, just as Sutekh's enormous longevity becomes a nightmare for him, trapped first in his 'tomb' and then in the time tunnel. Guy Boothby's Pharos the Egyptian has been cursed with eternal life as punishment for his involvement in the Biblical exodus. The villain of Hammer's *The Curse of the Mummy's Tomb* similarly seeks an end to his endless life. Ayesha in *She*, Sosra in Doyle's 'Ring of Thoth', and Imhotep in Universal's *The Mummy* are all separated from their lovers for eternity, and each has a different plan to reunite with them. Universal's sequels reuse the romance plot, with the additional danger of the desire of the 'high priest' for the leading lady. *The Mummy's Ghost* adds the reincarnation device, with the Princess Ananka reborn as the leading lady.

The direct source of *Pyramids of Mars*, Hammer's *The Mummy*, has only vestiges of the love story: the hero's wife is, through mere coincidence, the twin of Kharis' beloved princess, which disrupts Bey's control over an otherwise obediently violent servant. Otherwise, the movies are firmly focused on the curse narrative. This suits 1970s **Doctor Who**, which is set in a world largely devoid of sexuality and romance. Heterosexual desire surfaces now and again, mostly in the form of married couples, but it never drives the narrative (with the exception of Jo and Cliff Jones' courtship in *The Green Death* (1973)), and Sarah never shows any interest in either. Were Sarah to fall in love, it would surely result in her exit from the series, as it does for Jo and Leela, who have stepped out of this asexual, aromantic realm[179].

And, as is often the case, Sarah is the only female character in the story[180]. One reason for the paucity of female characters in 70s **Doctor Who** is that Robert Holmes disliked killing them[181]. Given the gruesome death toll in many of the stories he scripted or script-edited, and the sexualised violence in some of Hammer's movies, I think we can be thankful for Holmes' chivalry: a **Doctor Who** in which terrified women were pursued and strangled would be a **Doctor Who** punctuated by proxy rapes. (As it is, the Australian Broadcasting Corporation snipped some of the intense distress of Namin and Warlock as they were killed[182].)

More positively, the lack of romantic subplots meant that girls and women viewing the show could watch a young woman doing things other than preparing for marriage – such as expertly firing a rifle, as

---

[179] Even when she falls in love in **The Sarah Jane Adventures** (*The Wedding of Sarah Jane Smith*, 2009), it's a setup by the Trickster, intended to end her career as Earth's protector.

[180] Of 13 Holmes-edited stories, Sarah is the only woman in five: *The Sontaran Experiment*, *Revenge of the Cybermen*, *Planet of Evil*, *Pyramids* (all 1975), and *The Masque of Mandragora* (1976). (She would be the only woman in *The Android Invasion* (1975) but for the appearance of Tessa the technician in episode 4.) Even in stories with major female characters – *Robot* (1974-75)'s Miss Winters, *The Ark in Space*'s Vira, *Terror of the Zygons* (1975)'s Sister Lamont, *The Seeds of Doom* (1976)'s Amelia Ducat – those are the **only** other women besides Sarah.

[181] Wiggins, 'Infotext', *Pyramids of Mars*.

[182] These scenes were startling when I finally got to see them, if only because the censored Australian version of the story was so familiar.

Sarah does in *Pyramids*. But that's an outstanding moment of heroine-ism: Sarah may be 'very plucky'[183], but she still spends most of her time receiving exposition from the Doctor, and takes her turn being carried by a mummy in her flowing dress, as if on a movie poster.

'Superstitious Savage!'

The 1960s and 1970s in Britain were a time of anxiety around the continuing loss of the Empire and about the arrival of non-white immigrants from former British colonies, reflected in the nervous humour of series such as **Curry and Chips** (1969), **Mind Your Language** (ITV, 1977-1979) and **Love Thy Neighbour** (ITV, 1972-1976). Some **Doctor Who** stories overtly reference this period: *The Mutants* (1972) concerns the end of the Earth Empire's 500-year occupation of, and exploitation of, the planet Solos. (By contrast, *Colony in Space* (1971) and *Death to the Daleks* (1974) take the human exploitation of planets populated by 'primitives' as a given.)

Other stories draw on earlier paranoia about imperial subjects and immigrants. The vicious caricature of the Chinese as secretive, criminal, and weird was most prominently promulgated by the **Fu Manchu** novels by Sax Rohmer (author of *The Green Eyes of Bast*) and their TV and film adaptations, including the 60s flicks starring Christopher Lee which are partly the source of *The Talons of Weng-Chiang*[184]. Perhaps fortunately, modern Egypt and Egyptians are

---

[183] Episode 2.

[184] Rohmer admitted 'I know nothing about the Chinese' (quoted by Douglas G Greene in his introduction to *The Insidious Dr. Fu-Manchu*, New York, Dover, 1997, p vi). Rohmer apparently used whatever 'Eastern' details came to mind, including repeatedly describing Fu as resembling Pharaoh Seti I and giving him an

largely irrelevant to *Pyramids of Mars*[185]. The only Egyptians in the story are Scarman's workers, including Ahmed, whose one line is delivered by Palestinian-born actor Vic Tablian[186]; and Ibrahim Namin, played by Irish actor Peter Mayock[187], dead by the end of episode 1.

Doctor Who fans are understandably reluctant to acknowledge racism in the series, especially in well-loved and highly-regarded stories like *Talons*[188]. While *Talons* wears its contempt for the Chinese on its sleeve — to the extent that it was not screened in Ontario after consultation with the Chinese immigrant community

---

Egyptian slave woman named Kâramanèh. In the movie *The Brides of Fu Manchu* (1966), Fu's appropriately exotic secret hideout is an Ancient Egyptian temple.

[185] Perhaps it's fortunate, also, that there are no black characters (a rara avis in 70s **Doctor Who** in any case). While people from neighbouring Nubia were part of Ancient Egyptian society at every level — servants, tutors, police, soldiers, priests, and pharaohs — movies set in Ancient Egypt tend to portray them solely as slaves. This relationship was apparently seen as so natural that Karloff's Imhotep is able to command a black man in modern Cairo.

[186] Credited in *Pyramids* as Vik Tablian. 'Vic Tablian', Internet Movie Database.

[187] 'Irish actor Peter Mayock as The Young Lieutenant in a scene...', RTE Archive; a review of the play 'Love and a Bottle' remarks 'in Peter Mayock Ireland has a true comedian' ('At the Dublin Theatre Festival', *Punch*, 19 October 1966, issue 6580, p597.)

[188] Vasquez, Joshua, 'The Moral Economy of **Doctor Who**: Forgiving Fans and the Objects of their Devotion'. Hansen, Christopher J, *Ruminations, Peregrinations, and Regenerations*, pp239-40. In a possibly unintentional pun, Vasquez refers to the 'canonisation' of Robert Holmes by fans.

there[189] – *Pyramids* is lucky in that the racism in its DNA has become somewhat diluted. This is not to say that it's absent: *Pyramids* still has its fanatical foreigner and the hidden, exotic danger he brings into Britain – a stereotype of Arab immigrants all too familiar today.

But while the sixties Fu Manchu movies replicate Sax Rohmer's crude fantasies, Hammer's *The Mummy* gives Ibrahim Namin's forerunner Mehemet Bey a thought-provoking encounter with archaeologist John Banning (Peter Cushing), in which the dignified Egyptian argues that Banning's profession involves 'desecration': 'You force your way in, you remove the remains of the long-dead kings, and send them to places like the British Museum, where thousands of people can stare at them.' For his part, Banning deliberately provokes Bey in the hope the Egyptian will give himself away – calling Karnak a 'third-rate god' whose followers' 'standard of intelligence must have been remarkably low' – much as the Doctor often needles his foes into boasting about their plans or revealing themselves (Klieg and Davros both demonstrate their megalomania at the Doctor's prompting). There are no such tricks to be played on Sutekh.

In the *Mummy* films the original tomb violators, Imhotep and Kharis, are cursed for disturbing the peace of the dead. Opening an Egyptian tomb and removing its treasures to the UK or the US triggers a similar curse, but the 'high priest' and the mummy are the story's villains, and the hero and heroine will escape in the end. The movies might contrast an entrepreneur's crass commercialism with an archaeologist's loftier motives (as in *The Curse of the*

---

[189] 'Overseas Overview', DWM #71, p28.

Mummy's Tomb), but almost nowhere is archaeology itself questioned[190] – any more than Britain's occupation is. Banning taunts Bey: 'The history of your country is steeped in violence.' Somehow, the aggression of France and Britain have become Egyptian aggression, represented by the 'high priest' and the mummy. The streamlined retelling that is *Pyramids* has no room for such considerations: Namin is dispatched without ever having a scene with the Doctor.

Pyramids avoids all these issues by making Sutekh the Destroyer an absolute existential threat, not just to 'unbelievers', but to everything alive. He is not a villain with a point of view to be considered, nor flaws which can be exploited by the Doctor's clever tongue. He is a nuclear device, a black hole; there is no moral argument to be had; he must be stopped. As in Egyptian Gothic literature and the movies, British men find themselves largely helpless in the face of an ancient, mystic Eastern power. Even the Doctor defeats Sutekh by sheer luck – or rather, by being as well-equipped for his task as Perseus. Without his respiratory bypass system and his TARDIS, all would have been lost.

---

[190] As well as Bey's speech, the fortune-teller Haiti in *The Mummy's Shroud* takes pity on the leading lady and tells her how to avoid the curse: apologise to the mummy for desecrating the tomb.

'YES, BUT EGYPTOLOGY AND MARS?'

Why is it *Pyramids of Mars*, and not, say, 'Pyramids of Venus', or 'Pyramids of the Moon'? In Lewis Greifer's initial storyline, scientists plan to grow grain on the surface of Earth's moon; for unclear reasons, Seth contaminates the rocket-load of seedlings with an organism or substance which will, somehow, 'erode the moon and so destroy the life cycle of the Earth'[191].

For that matter, why isn't it 'Pyramid of Mars', singular, as mentioned in the dialogue? Presumably the name derives from the earlier version of the story, developed between Holmes and Greifer in July 1974, in which the Osirans were originally Martians, whose visit to Earth inspired Egyptian religion[192]. Certainly 'Pyramids', plural, is more evocative, suggesting an otherworldly equivalent of the landscape of Giza with its triplet of pyramids and accompanying Great Sphinx. It's a shame we never get to see the Martian pyramid from the outside – was there more Osiran architecture on Mars?

Marcus Scarman wrote to his brother Laurence to tell him he had discovered a 'blind pyramid [...] and believed it contained a mastaba'[193]. Mastabas – large brick or stone structures which covered the underground tombs of Egypt's earliest times – are certainly plentiful in Saqqara. However, I'm at a loss to explain what a 'blind pyramid' is. It's possible that Holmes was trying to describe the shape of a mastaba, the inward-sloping walls of which make it look like the very bottom of a pyramid (a 'blunt pyramid'?).

---

[191] Pixley, 'Archive', p33.
[192] Pixley, 'Archive', p28.
[193] Episode 2.

Perhaps he simply meant a blind passage, ending in a wall which Scarman suspected concealed a tomb.

Mars, of course, was associated with the idea of extraterrestrial life for decades before **Doctor Who** contributed its own malevolent Martians, the Ice Warriors (*The Ice Warriors*, 1967) and the Flood (*The Waters of Mars*, 2009). During the 19th century, the planet was extensively observed by astronomers, who thought they saw oceans and clouds. In 1854 scientist and philosopher William Whewell speculated on the possible life forms that could inhabit Mars[194]. Astronomer Giovanni Schiaparelli[195] first mistakenly identified natural water-carrying 'channels' on the planet's surface in 1877; his 'canali' were misunderstood as artificially-made canals by English speakers[196]. Astronomer Percival Lowell, who even mapped the imaginary canals – the product of a simple optical illusion – wrote about them in his *Mars* in 1895, suggesting the Martians were engaged in a last-ditch attempt to irrigate their dying world. Two years later, HG Wells published one of SF's seminal works, *The War of the Worlds*, in which Martians attempt to colonise Earth, successfully overthrow humanity, and are only defeated in the end by their susceptibility to terrestrial microbes. (Lowell would continue to write about the canals until the installation of a 60-inch telescope at Mount Wilson Observatory, the largest so far, made it possible to observe the planet's surface more clearly.)

---

[194] Whewell, William, *The Plurality of Worlds: An Essay*, p187.

[195] Sadly, a Mars lander named in Schiaparelli's honour crashed during the writing of this essay, on 19 October 2016.

[196] Asimov, Isaac, *Extraterrestrial Civilizations*.

The Ancient Egyptians were expert astronomers and were aware of the retrograde motion of Mars – the way that, as Earth passes Mars in its orbit, Mars temporarily travels east-to-west in the sky before resuming its previous movement west-to-east. In the tomb of Seti I, an astronomical chart painted on the ceiling identifies Mars with the god Horus of the Horizon, depicting him as a falcon-headed man wearing a star on his head and standing in a boat, and notes: 'He travels backwards'. Later, in the Ptolemaic era, Mars would be called 'Horus the Red'. In Seti I's chart of the sky, Jupiter and Saturn were also identified with versions of Horus, while Set was assigned to the planet Mercury[197]. Coincidentally, the landscape revealed by the Viking missions, a featureless red plain, suggests the Red Land, the deserts outside the fertile Nile valley which were the provenance of Set.

Science fiction began drawing connections between Mars and Ancient Egypt in the late 19th century[198]. In 1898, in what can be called an early piece of fanfiction, *Edison's Conquest of Mars* – an unofficial sequel to an unauthorised re-telling of *War of the Worlds* – US writer Garrett P Serviss dispatches Thomas Edison and other real, living scientists to Mars, where they learn that the Martians have invaded Earth in the past and, impressed by Earth's mountains, built the pyramids in imitation of them: 'It was not the

[197] Parker, RA, 'Ancient Egyptian Astronomy'. *Philosophical Transactions of the Royal Society of London. Series A, Mathematical and Physical Sciences*, 276 (1257), p60.

[198] This chapter is indebted to correspondence in *Fortean Times* addressing speculation as to whether **Doctor Who** was the first text to link Mars and pyramids. (Cornell, Paul, 'Doctor Who: Forteana in Time and Space'. *Fortean Times* #318, p38. 'Letters: Pyramids on Mars'. *Fortean Times* #320, p69.)

work of puny man, as many an engineer had declared that it could not be, but the work of these giants of Mars.'[199] As we'll see, he would not be the last person to attribute the pyramids to extraterrestrial architects. The plot of *Pharaoh's Broker* (1899) by Ellsworth Douglass concerns an American speculator who travels via 'gravity projectile' to Mars, where he discovers a fanciful version of Ancient Egypt which has arisen independently of the historical one on Earth – complete with pharaoh and parallel Joseph (though, surprisingly, no pyramids).

Stanley G Weinbaum's[200] 1934 story 'A Martian Odyssey'[201] is noted for being the earliest SF story to portray aliens as having different minds to human beings, with astronaut Dick Jarvis struggling to communicate with a Martian named Tweel as they share adventures. One encounter involves unintelligent silicon-based creatures which built neat pyramids out of bricks of their own waste matter. More significantly, in the less well-known sequel, 'Valley of Dreams' (1934), Jarvis learns that Tweel's people call themselves 'Thoth', and that the visit of the bird-like Martians to Earth thousands of years ago led to the invention of writing[202].

Brothers Earl Andrew Binder and Otto Binder would contribute a series of 10 stories about alien pyramids to the pages of pulp

---

[199] Serviss, Garrett P, *Edison's Conquest of Mars* p197.

[200] A crater on Mars bears Weinbaum's name.

[201] Weinbaum, Stanley Grauman, 'A Martian Odyssey'.

[202] It's unclear whether Tweel is **a** Thoth, or whether his people are collectively **the** Thoth. Although these Martians don't build pyramids, they do have monumental buildings: Jarvis describes the structures of their city as 'Gargantuan!' Weinbaum, Stanley Grauman, 'Valley of Dreams'.

magazine *Thrilling Wonder Stories* (under their joint pseudonym, Gordon A Giles), beginning in 1937 with 'Via Etherline', in which explorers discover Egyptian-style pyramids on Mars and throughout the solar system. Once again the idea that the Egyptians could not themselves have built the pyramids comes into play: eventually the heroes discover that the pyramids were part of an immense gravity machine, which was used in an effort to push a planet out of a dangerously eccentric orbit close to Mars, only to inadvertently destroy it, creating the asteroid belt[203].

Real-life spacecraft on their way to Mars would have been in the news around the time *Pyramids* was being hatched. The Viking landers, which would look for signs of life, had been planned for 1973; their launch was postponed to 1975 after NASA's budget was slashed in 1970[204]. After the landers sent back images of the planet's surface, the mis-seen canals were replaced by a new generation of imaginary features. Perhaps inevitably, given the planet's science-fictional heritage, a pyramid has recently been added to the long list[205].

As with Lowell's hypothetical Martians, the invaders of *War of the Worlds* are driven by the need to find a new home to replace their

---

[203] The stories were combined into a 1971 novel, *Puzzle of the Space Pyramids* (published under another of the brothers' pen-names, Eando Binder). Simon Bucher-Jones discusses the discredited theory that the Asteroid Belt is the remains of a Fifth Planet at length in *The Black Archive #5: Image of the Fendahl* (2016).
[204] 'Space Economies'. *The Canberra Times*, 17 January 1970, p4.
[205] Freeman, David, 'Mars "Pyramid" Seen By NASA Rover Isn't Quite What It Seems'. *The Huffington Post*, 26 July 2015.

freezing, drying planet[206]. This was also the Osirans' motivation in the July 1974 version of *Pyramids*: meeting with Lewis Greifer, Robert Holmes made several suggestions, one of which was that the Osirans visited Earth because Mars could no longer support life[207]. Unlike Wells' Martians, however, Greifer's Osirans turned back when they discovered intelligent life was present on Earth, placing themselves into suspended animation, waiting for the human race to develop the technology to visit them on Mars and assist in the planet's regeneration. First, however, they had to overcome Seth and his lieutenant Sebek, who wanted to conquer the Earth, eventually imprisoning them in Egypt. A different suggestion came from Barry Letts: the Egyptian gods were members of multiple species that had travelled from beyond our solar system, retreating to Mars when they realised Earth was inhabited.

In the televised version of the story, it's never explicitly stated why the Eye of Horus, which keeps Sutekh imprisoned, is on Mars. However, it's not difficult to guess: this way, the transmitter is firmly out of the evil Osiran's reach.

---

[206] Wells, HG, *The War of the Worlds*, p2.
[207] Pixley, 'Archive', p28.

'PYRAMID POWER'

Victorian Egyptomania coincided with, and overlapped with, a boom in interest in the occult: spiritualism and séances, reincarnation and psychic powers. The Theosophical Society and the Hermetic Order of the Golden Dawn, secret societies involving initiation and ritual magic, believed that the Ancient Egyptians had possessed advanced magical powers and sought to rediscover them[208]. They argued that the sceptics would soon be proved wrong as science found explanations for supernatural phenomena[209]. In *Dracula*, van Helsing lists some of the interests of the time:

> '"Ah, it is the fault of our science that it wants to explain all; and if it explain not, then it says there is nothing to explain. But yet we see around us every day the growth of new beliefs, which think themselves new; and which are yet but the old, which pretend to be young – like the fine ladies at the opera. I suppose now you do not believe in corporeal transference. No? Nor in materialisation. No? Nor in astral bodies. No? Nor in the reading of thought. No? Nor in hypnotism—"
>
> '"Yes," I said. "Charcot has proved that pretty well."'[210]

The medical studies of hypnosis by pioneering French neurologist Jean-Martin Charcot had brought 'mesmerism' across the border from the paranormal and into science. So why, the argument ran,

---

[208] Luckhurst, *The Mummy's Curse*, p213.
[209] Luckhurst, *The Mummy's Curse*, p233.
[210] Stoker, Bram, *Dracula*, p219.

couldn't other mental powers turn out to be real? Roger Luckhurst describes 'a twilight zone where infection, psychical suggestion, the exertion of the magical will and radioactive particles coexist in the vanishing point between science and the occult.'[211] To put it another way, hypnosis, radiation, psychic powers, and the mummy's curse were all science fiction.

The Jewel of Seven Stars characterises the mysterious powers of Ancient Egypt as not magical but scientific:

> 'the Egyptians knew sciences, of which today, despite all our advantages, we are profoundly ignorant [...] these old miracle-workers probably understood some practical way of using other forces, and amongst them the forces of light that at present we do not dream of [...] That Magic Coffer of Queen Tera is probably a magic box in more ways than one. It may – possibly it does – contain forces that we wot not of.'[212]

Carter Lupton writes that *Jewel* 'essentially brought the fictional mummy story into the 20th century, attempting to meld notions of mysticism [...] with the progressiveness of modern science.'[213]

This is exactly the approach that **Doctor Who** would take decades later, giving the supernatural a scientific gloss. Generally speaking, for modern viewers, if something has a scientific basis (even a gobbledygook one, if it's presented with convincing authority) it's more plausible, realer, lending the horror an edge unavailable to

---

[211] Luckhurst, *The Mummy's Curse*, pp174-75.
[212] Stoker, *Dracula*, pp130-1.
[213] Lupton, '"Mummymania" for the Masses', p28.

pure fantasy. 'Embalmed, eviscerated corpses' can't stalk and kill –
but machines might[214].

The Victorian occultists often claimed that they were the recipients
of a tradition of secret knowledge handed down through the
centuries. This seems to actually be the case with Sutekh's human
followers:

> 'The gods have returned. I, Ibrahim Namin, servant of the
> true faith, rejoice in their power [...] The servants of the All-
> Powerful have arisen. When the temple is cleansed of all
> unbelievers, the High One himself will come among us[215].
> This is how it was written.'[216]

(Interesting that he says 'the gods', 'their power', plural – perhaps
referring to allies of Sutekh amongst the Osirans? Unlike the
Doctor, Namin doesn't know that Sutekh is the last of his kind.)
Later, he addresses the figure he believes is Sutekh:

> 'I, Ibrahim Namin, and all my forebears have served you
> faithfully through the thousands of years that you have
> slept. We have guarded the secret of your tomb.'

---

[214] Episode 1. The ethics and hazards of robots programmed to kill
for military purposes are a current controversy. See for example
'Autonomous Weapons: an Open Letter from AI & Robotics
Researchers'.
[215] As well as 'the Destroyer', the Egyptians called Set 'Great of
Power' and 'Lord of Heaven', which are not bad matches for
Namin's 'All-Powerful' and 'High One'. Leitz, *Lexikon der
Ägyptischen Götter*, pp667-668.
[216] Episode 1.

A cult which lasted this long, especially in secret, would be an accomplishment that nuclear semioticians would envy: one proposed solution to the long-term problem of nuclear waste storage is to create an 'atomic priesthood', an organisation which would pass down knowledge of the dangerous site through the ages[217].

'The Riddle of the Osirans'

What does Namin hope to gain from aiding Sutekh? The Osiran has probably promised him power, much as he promises to give the Doctor the Earth as a 'plaything'[218]. Conceivably Namin is a nationalist who hopes to expel the foreign rulers from Egypt, turning their desire for Egyptian antiquities against them, with Sutekh's help. Philip J Turner characterises the god Set as a 'conman'[219], capable of sufficient charm to deceive his victims – as when Osiris not only attends a party thrown by Set, despite his suspicions of his power-hungry brother, but even goes along with Set's promise to give a beautiful wooden chest to whoever fits inside it. The chest, of course, becomes Osiris's coffin, as Set and his followers shut him inside and throw it into the Nile[220].

---

[217] Musch, Sebastian, 'The Atomic Priesthood and Nuclear Waste Management-Religion: Religion, Sci-fi Literature and the End of our Civilization'. *Zygon: Journal of Religion and Science*, 51 (3), 2016.

[218] Episode 4.

[219] Turner, Philip J, 'Thoughts on Seth the Conman' in Price, Campbell, Roger Forshaw, Andrew Chamberlain and Paul Nicholson, eds, *Mummies, Magic and Medicine*. The thought of Gabriel Woolf doing Sutekh's persuasive voice sends a shiver down my spine.

[220] Plutarch, *Moralia*.

In Universal's *The Mummy*, Imhotep knows where his beloved's tomb is and leads the archaeologists to it. Could Namin and/or other cultists have done something similar for Scarman? It seems more likely that Sutekh's followers had lost the location of the tomb, or never knew it – otherwise they could have rescued their god themselves.

In fact, it's possible Sutekh was simply forgotten for thousands of years. Like the Victorian occultists, the cult of Sutekh could be a modern institution founded after the decipherment of hieroglyphs in the early 19th century made records of the god's existence available once more. This new cult would naturally call itself the inheritors of the old – its 'forebears'. (Whether the cult is old or new, it's not impossible that Namin is the **sole** worshipper of Sutekh on Earth.)

That all this isn't spelled out on screen is not a flaw in the story – rather, it's fun to speculate, to fill in background details that just weren't necessary for Robert Holmes's no-nonsense narrative. Although there are some elements that leave the viewer puzzled after multiple viewings: what's the source of the Osiran technology we see? Surely the Osirans didn't bury Sutekh with the equipment he would need to free himself, including the servitors and the missile? (Or perhaps they did; movie mummies are always buried with the means to bring them to life.) And why bring the equipment to Scarman's English estate, rather than building and launching the rocket from Egypt – say, from a secluded spot in the desert?

Again it's entertaining to speculate: perhaps the aliens did indeed leave robots behind, to maintain and guard Sutekh's tomb – much as there are robots guarding the pyramid on Mars – and these have malfunctioned or been sabotaged at some stage. Or perhaps Sutekh has directed the manufacture of these items – probably primitive by his standards, but adequate. (The robots on Mars may be more sophisticated than the ones on Earth; they must be able to not just answer questions, but answer untruthfully, which requires some level of intelligence. The robots directed by Namin and Scarman display, and need, only the ability to follow commands.) Namin, acting as Scarman's agent (the 'animated cadaver' could never have shown himself) might have had access to funds, materials, and equipment in Britain that he could not access in Egypt.

It's tempting to say that Sutekh travels through the time tunnel at the story's climax, rather than starting his promised revenge on the spot, because the plot requires him to do so. It's not that he wants to begin his destruction with his enemies; he believes the Doctor to be dead and Sarah to be trapped on Mars. Perhaps there's equipment in England that he needs. Or perhaps he plans to start his vengeance with the civilisation that foolishly freed him.

Finally, there's the 'dungeon crawl on Mars'[221], as both Sutekh and the Doctor must solve a series of logic puzzles to reach the Eye of Horus. Sarah remarks that it reminds her of 'the City of the Exxilons' from *Death to the Daleks*. In that instance, the Doctor deduces that the intelligence tests he (and the pursuing Daleks) must pass are intended to let through those who might have some

---

[221] Ciechanowski, Walt, and Andrew Peregrine, *The Fourth Doctor Sourcebook*, p62.

'knowledge or science' the Exxilons could make use of[222]. Similarly, the Cybermen are waiting for 'superior intellects', keeping others out with the puzzles required to enter their tomb on Telos.

The purpose of the tricks and traps in *Pyramids* is less clear: if Sutekh is never to be released, why allow access to the Eye at all? I can think of two reasons: firstly, maintenance. Secondly, as I speculated earlier, there might have come a time when the Osirans needed Sutekh. The puzzles act as locks to his prison; the key is a mind capable of solving them – which, they assumed, would be an Osiran mind.

'Some Sort of Mesmeric Influence'

In the late-Victorian era, there was a struggle over the legitimacy of hypnosis, which included a general panic over how 'mesmeric influence' might be used by dastardly Jews or Arabs to control the weaker wills of British men and women. Inevitably, mind control became one of the stocks in trade of fictional Eastern villains. As Roger Luckhurst notes, 'every villain of the Egyptian Gothic has access to [...] powers [...] foolishly dismissed by Western science'[223]. Svengali, the Jewish caricature of George du Maurier's novel *Trilby* (1895), lent his name to the English language as a term for a sinister hypnotist[224]. (Warner Brothers made a movie of the story the year before Universal released *The Mummy*.)

The dastardly hypnotist often possesses eerie eyes that reflect light red or green, like the eyes of a cat or a snake. Pharos the Egyptian

---

[222] *Death to the Daleks* episode 4.

[223] Luckhurst, *The Mummy's Curse*, pp212-13.

[224] For more on *Trilby* and the history of hypnosis in fiction see Dennis, Jon, *The Black Archive #6: Ghost Light* (2016).

('His eyes shone in his head like living coals and seemed to burn into my brain'[225]) and the awful formless villain of Richard Marsh's *The Beetle* (1897) hypnotise their prey. Dracula, whose eyes are red, puts his victims into a trance. The killer in Rohmer's *The Green Eyes of Bast* has 'blazing', 'fiery' cat's-eyes; Fu Manchu has 'long, magnetic eyes of the true cat-green' and uses drugs and hypnosis. In *The Talons of Weng-Chiang* Li H'Sen Chang's eyes literally flash as he mesmerises his victims. In Universal's *The Mummy*, Imhotep holds Helen entranced with his gaze; in an effects shot, his eyes appear out of shadow, making them seem to glow[226]. She-who-must-be-obeyed destroys her rival in love with a look:

> 'Ayesha said nothing, she made no sound, she only drew herself up, stretched out her arm, and, her tall veiled frame quivering like an aspen leaf, appeared to look fixedly at her victim. Even as she did so Ustane put her hands to her head, uttered one piercing scream, turned round twice, and then fell backwards with a thud – prone upon the floor. Both Leo and myself rushed to her – she was stone dead – blasted into death by some mysterious electric agency or overwhelming will-force whereof the dread **She** had command.'[227]

This is strikingly similar to the blast from Sutekh's eyes, accompanied by a poisonous green light, with which the Osiran strikes down Scarman and torments the Doctor. Capable of both blasting his victims with his gaze and of controlling their minds,

---

[225] Boothby, Guy. *Pharos, the Egyptian*, p230.
[226] Perhaps a more advanced version of the shots in Universal's *Dracula* (1931) in which light falls across the Count's hypnotic eyes.
[227] Haggard, H Rider, *She*, p158.

Sutekh has inherited not just the Egyptian concept of the powerful eye, but the fear of Svengali.

'Mental Projection of That Force is Beyond Imagination'

The flourishing occultism of the Victorian era was paralleled by a boom in interest in the paranormal in the late 1960s and early 1970s. Paperback and part-work magazine titles of the time give an idea of the range of out-of-the-ordinary interests: *Witchcraft for All* (1969), *Man, Myth and Magic* (1970), *Black Magic Today* (1971), *Dream Telepathy: Experiments in Nocturnal ESP* (1973), *Investigating UFOs* (1974), *The Psychic Scene* (1974), *Mysterious Britain* (1974). Documentaries such as *The Power of the Witch* (1971) and *UFOs: Past, Present, and Future* (1974) fed the public's taste for the unknown. As in the 19th century, some of these ideas were given a boost of believability through their connection with science. UFOs and alien visitors were a fringe idea, but they were a **scientific** idea, and the Search for Extra-terrestrial Intelligence, SETI, was a genuine scientific effort.

Ideas in this niche between science and pseudoscience were ideal material for science fiction, and fertile ground for **Doctor Who**, in which a scientific, rationalist attitude has always been more important than actual scientific accuracy. Any gap between what's realistic given current scientific understanding and a needed plot element can be filled by an appeal to the sufficiently advanced science of the Time Lords or other high-tech aliens, or of the distant human future. For example, in 20th-century **Doctor Who**, psychic powers may be brought about by selective breeding (*The Face of Evil* (1977)), by the proximity of a time fissure (*Image of the Fendahl* (1977)) or the energy released when living worlds are destroyed (*The Pirate Planet* (1978)), or they may simply be innate (it's not clear in *The Dæmons* (1971) whether Olive Hawthorne has paranormal abilities or just a strong and unusual mind, but poor Professor Clegg in *Planet of the Spiders* (1974) is certainly psychically gifted). The power of the mind can be enhanced (*Spiders* again) or even reified (*Snakedance* (1983)) by crystals. In each case, telepathy, precognition, and other powers are not supernatural, but are presented as science. Even machines can make use of them: in *The Pirate Planet*, K9 can follow the Mentiads' 'psycho-spoor'. It's only natural, therefore, that highly advanced aliens like the Time Lords and the Osirans would have their own psychic powers, with Sutekh reading the Doctor's mind and containing the gelignite explosion through psychokinesis.

For *Pyramids of Mars*, the most important non-fiction is probably Erich von Däniken's enormously popular *Chariots of the Gods? Unsolved Mysteries of the Past*, published in 1968. A version of the 1970 West German documentary based on *Chariots* was shown in British cinemas in late 1970 and early 1971[228]. In von Däniken's rather vague speculations, frequently based on incorrect data[229], hardly any ancient culture on Earth has been left untouched by the influence of alien astronauts – from 8,000-year-old rock art in

---

[228] For example, Manchester cinema listings in *The Guardian*, 20 February 1971, p6.

[229] To give a few examples off the top of my head: Egyptian prehistory is well-documented, and the culture and technology of the pyramid-builders did not 'appear suddenly and without transition' (p94); far from wood being rare and thus unavailable for construction use (p95), it was a commonplace material; there are examples of wooden artefacts in countless museums, along with the ropes that von Däniken claims were 'non-existent' (p99).

Algeria, to the pyramids of Egypt built around 2500 BCE, to the pyramids of the Central American city of Teotihuacan, which flourished around 100-550 CE, to the giant statues of Easter Island in the Atlantic, erected around 1250-1500 CE. This comprehensive interference is less like the one-off contact of *Pyramids* and more like the deliberate engineering of human evolution in *Image of the Fendahl* or the repeated acceleration of human technology in *City of Death*.

Doctor Who was naturally not the only British TV show to tap into this zeitgeist. The ITV anthology **Mystery and Imagination** (1966-1970) adapted *The Jewel of Seven Stars* as *Curse of the Mummy* (1970). The BBC's space opera **Blake's 7** did its own version with telepath Cally in place of Margaret Trelawney, possessed by an ancient alien entity (*Sarcophagus*, 1980). The six-part series **Sexton Blake and the Demon God** (BBC, 1978), produced by Barry Letts, concerned an Ancient Egyptian artefact, a stolen mummy, and a cult led by a Middle Eastern villain with the unlikely name of Hubba Pasha[230].

The Ace in **Ace of Wands** (Thames Television, 1970-1972) was Tarot, a stage magician with genuine psychic powers. The four-part story *The Power of Atep* (Victor Pemberton, 1972) name-checks the 'Treasures of Tutankhamun' exhibition held at the British Museum the same year as its broadcast, and appears to draw on that more than it does on the cinematic mummy[231]. Atep, we learn, was high

---

[230] Huckvale, *Touchstones of Gothic Horror*, p51.
[231] Another story, *The Eye of Ra* (1971), now lost, appears to have used some Egyptian trappings (including stage magician and show consultant Ali Bongo dressed as a mummy) in a story otherwise

priest and court magician to Thutmosis II; his mummy is stolen from the British Museum by Tarot's former stage partner, Qabal, who wants Atep's power for himself, as well as revenge on Tarot. Reading the words of 'The Book of Atep' activates paranormal occurrences, but doesn't animate Atep's mummy. In fact, despite the considerable psychic power that Atep and his followers apparently wield – using séances to overwhelm the minds of Tarot and his psychically gifted assistant Mikki, and creating a psychokinetic 'poltergeist' – in the end Tarot beats Qabal in a battle of stage magic and dismisses Atep as a 'charlatan'. The viewer is left unclear whether they have witnessed real paranormal power or mere stage illusions.

In mummy movies, sceptics are the ones who perish, while the hero moves from initial disbelief to accepting the warnings he receives[232]. Perhaps this is why **Ace of Wands** only half-debunks Atep's power. In *Pyramids*, the Doctor knows from the start that Sutekh is real and infinitely dangerous (contrast the Fendahl, which was mythological even to the Time Lords), although he initially dismisses Sarah's sighting of the robot mummies. The scepticism is left to Dr Warlock, who rejects Namin's threatening warning about 'ancient powers' as 'ancient balderdash', and Laurence Scarman, who cannot accept what's been done to his brother and attributes Marcus's state to 'some sort of mesmeric influence'[233]. Both perish – although only Laurence could be said to have brought his fate upon himself, by trying to rescue Marcus. In *Pyramids*, everyone

---

unrelated to Egypt. Pixley, Andrew, 'Viewing Notes', Ace of Wands DVD, 2007.

[232] Day, *The Mummy's Curse*, p67.

[233] *Pyramids of Mars* episodes 1, 3.

except the Doctor and his companion is doomed, with the exception of the Egyptian workers who have the sense to bolt the moment they see the Eye of Horus burst into red light in the tomb[234]. In fact, poor Warlock, who sleeps through the Doctor's explanation of Sutekh, has no reason to believe anything preternatural is occurring until a mummy walks into the room and kills him; he enters in a thriller and exits in a horror movie.

It's Marcus Scarman's scepticism, of course, that first imperils the Earth. Despite the warnings in Sutekh's tomb, I think there are two reasons he proceeds. One is simply ambition: 'I've come too far to turn back now.' The other is that he has derided Ahmed, his alarmed assistant, as a 'superstitious savage'[235]; if he shows doubt or fear, he brings into question whether the British really are more rational and civilised than the 'degenerate' Egyptians and whether the occupation really is for Egypt's own good.

Scarman, of course, is from a nation in which bickering occultists threatened to zap one another[236] and in which rumours of mummy curses thrived well before the opening of Tut's tomb[237]. In fact, his workers came from a culture whose long familiarity with ancient burials had bred contempt. Sir William Wilde, who visited Egypt in 1838, described smoking his pipe beside a campfire fuelled by his Arab guides with the contents of 'mummy-pots' (canopic jars?) and

---

[234] Keep an eye on the last man to enter the tomb. The non-speaking extra turns and leaves again with the perfect equanimity you might expect of someone not being paid enough to do more.
[235] Episode 1.
[236] Luckhurst, *The Mummy's Curse*, p213.
[237] Not to mention a nation developing an elaborate (and convenient) pseudoscience of race.

pieces of coffins[238]. It's likely Ahmed and Co were equally blasé about the ancients. What's remarkable is not the Egyptians' frightened response to the Eye of Horus; it's Marcus Scarman's failure to believe what is in front of his own rational, educated, supposedly superior eyes.

'The Wars of the Gods'

In **Ace of Wands**, only certain individuals are gifted with paranormal powers. **The Tomorrow People** (Thames Television, 1973-79) never really explored its central, disturbing premise: that the human race will inevitably be replaced by *Homo superior*, a new species with multiple psychic powers, who will 'take over, stop wars, and put the world in order'[239]. Their 'special powers' are scientific: the natural outcome of evolution. Rather than taking over from the 'saps', the Tomorrow People dealt with various threats from space and time.

The story *Worlds Away* (1975) reveals that Egypt's pyramids were constructed by aliens, the Khultan, former rulers of the Earth, who wear masks closely resembling the head of the god Anubis. The Great Pyramid contains what's left of a 'psi-damping transmitter', which suppressed the natural psionic powers of human beings. Galactic ambassador Timus remarks that 'the apex of this pyramid will exactly bisect the land and water masses of this planet [...] It was essential if the structure was to perform its function.'[240] In other words, the psi-dampener must be exactly centred in order to

---

[238] Wilde, Sir William Robert, *Narrative of a Voyage to Madeira, Teneriffe, and Along the Shores of the Mediterranean*, p66.
[239] **The Tomorrow People:** *The Slaves of Jedikiah*, Episode 3.
[240] **The Tomorrow People:** *Worlds Away*, Episode 1.

broadcast to every point on the globe. This is a clever use of von Däniken, who asks: 'Is it a coincidence that a meridian running through the pyramid divides continents and oceans into two exactly equal halves?'[241] (Alas, **every** meridian, or line of longitude, exactly bisects the continents and oceans.)

The idea that pyramids of Giza (or Teotihuacan, or Peru) could not have been built by the societies of their time is a central idea in 'alien astronauts' fiction and non-fiction both. It dates back to the time of Victorian Egyptomania; the first known alternative suggestion for the pyramid builders (Noah and his sons) was made in 1859 by John Taylor in *The Great Pyramid: Why it Was Built and Who Built It*[242], and von Däniken credits his meridian factoid to Charles Piazzi Smith's *Our Inheritance in the Great Pyramid* (1864)[243].

That the pyramids were built by the Osirans is certainly implied in *Pyramids of Mars*, if never stated outright; although it's also possible that the Egyptians built their pyramids in imitation of Osiran architecture, or under Osiran direction. In **The Tomorrow People**, Timus says that the pyramids being erected by aliens is easier to believe than 'that they were built by ancient primitives with a few simple tools and their bare hands'. The Doctor says the same thing of a 'Peruvian temple' in *Death to the Daleks*: 'it's one of Earth's great mysteries, that no primitive man could possibly have built such a structure.'

---

[241] Von Däniken, *Chariots of the Gods?*, p97.
[242] Shermer, Michael, *The Skeptic Encyclopedia of Pseudoscience*, Volume One, pp406-07.
[243] Von Däniken, *Chariots of the Gods?*, p96.

It's a curious fact that the West has both looked to Ancient Egypt as a source of advanced science and has simultaneously dismissed the Egyptians as incapable of the fairly basic engineering needed to cut, move, and position large chunks of rock. For the Victorians, it allowed a bit of intellectual sleight-of-hand: the Ancient Egyptians were great, but they weren't Africans, they were **us** – our racial and/or cultural ancestors. The 20th-century update of the idea only retains the first part of the formula, as if to say, if **we** didn't build the pyramids, then no-one else did, either – at least, no other human beings.

The concept of aliens influencing human technological development was perfect for **Doctor Who**, a show in which both alien invaders and Earth's history were standard elements. But while von Däniken's hypothetical alien gods were benevolent, their **Who** equivalents were rather less so. Linx, the stranded Sontaran in *The Time Warrior* (1973-74), trades advanced weapons to Mediaeval brigands in exchange for the materials he needs to repair his spacecraft, heedless of the danger to humanity that such a leap forward in the technology of killing will cause. The Fendahl's skull, fallen to Earth in Kenya, has bent the evolution of the human brain to its own needs. In *City of Death* Scaroth, last of the Jagaroth, forces technological progress throughout human history in order to develop time travel and return through millions of years to his own spacecraft before its destruction – an explosion, which, paradoxically, sparked the beginning of life on Earth.

In the 20th-century series, *The Dæmons* brings us closest to the use of the idea in *Pyramids*, in which the visiting aliens have left their imprint in mythology – specifically, in the form of a Devil-like figure. 21st-century **Who** returns to this idea in *The Impossible Planet /*

The Satan Pit (2006), a story which shows the influence of both *Dæmons* and *Pyramids*: an archaeological dig puts Earth and more in danger by releasing an ancient, powerful, Satanic figure. 'The Beast' is voiced by Gabriel Woolf, who provided Sutekh's terrifying voice. The Beast's use of pieces of information about the base's crew to seem omniscient recalls the Master's manipulation of the inhabitants of Devil's End in *The Dæmons*. There's also an invocation of colonial fears in the form of the servile Ood ('They're born for it. Basic slave race,' quips their handler[244]) and their uprising – troubling because it's never properly explored or resolved, at least in this story[245].

In a speech mirroring the third Doctor's enumeration of horned supernatural beings in *The Dæmons*, and the fourth Doctor's listing of Sutekh's names throughout the cosmos ('Set, Satan, Sadok'[246]) the tenth Doctor says: 'You get representations of the Horned Beast right across the universe, in the myths and legends of a million worlds. Earth, Draconia, Velconsadine, Daemos. The Kaled god of war.'[247] Interestingly, the image of the horned deity seems to have entered Egyptian religion in the form of benevolent

---

[244] *The Impossible Planet.*

[245] Lindy A Orthia ('Sociopathetic Abscess or Yawning Chasm? The Absent Postcolonial Transition in **Doctor Who**'. *The Journal of Commonwealth Literature*, 45 (2), p8) critiques the eventual resolution of this problem in *Planet of the Ood* (2008), in which the Ood become the 'white man's burden' for the Doctor and Donna, who they all but worship as their saviours.

[246] The name 'Sadok' appears to be an invention of Robert Holmes. It suggests 'sadist'; in fact, as a child, I thought this must be the where the term came from. Pleasingly, there is a Spanish metal band called Sadok.

[247] *The Satan Pit.*

goddesses and gods such as Hathor, Khnum, and the supreme deity Amun-Re. As the Doctor and Olive Hawthorne remark, for humans, horns have always been a symbol of power – in this case, power for good.

'THE TIME OF THE OSIRANS IS LONG PAST'

When Russell T Davies re-opened the Cardiff Bay **Doctor Who** Exhibition in late 2008, a failure of organisation led to his being unexpectedly mobbed by fans in a small, tight space, trapped by an unending 'procession' of grownups and children wanting autographs and photographs. The exhibition had to be temporarily stopped so he could escape[248]. This incident is bizarrely like the experience in 1846 of Crown Prince Ibrahim of Egypt, who stepped into an exhibition in Birmingham and suddenly found himself being announced as one of the exhibits; the police had to get him out[249].

When Egyptians visited Europe in the late 19th century, they found not only that they themselves were stared at by Western crowds; they also discovered facsimiles of Egypt, like the mock Cairo street in the World Exhibition in Paris in 1889, complete with cosplay and realistic chaos and dirt. 'Their final embarrassment,' writes Timothy Mitchell, 'had been to enter the door of the mosque and discover that, like the rest of the street, it had been erected as what the Europeans called a façade.' Inside was a coffee shop with dancing girls[250].

This has been the fate of Egypt, especially Ancient Egypt, in Western literature, cinema, and television: to be a spectacle, a simulation, a veneer of Egyptian details propped up in front of Western fantasies of sex, treasure, and/or the fear of revenge.

---

[248] Davies, Russell T, and Benjamin Cook, *The Writer's Tale: The Final Chapter*, pp494-95.

[249] Mitchell, Timothy, *Colonising Egypt*, p4.

[250] Mitchell, *Colonising Egypt*, p1.

Carter Lupton describes Universal's *Mummy* as being made up of 'a mélange of elements from literature, popular culture, and historical reality'[251], without much in the way of authentic detail. The sequel, *The Mummy's Hand*, borrows a set from another movie, *Green Hell* (1940) – an Inca temple, complete with giant llama heads; one fake standing in for another. 'What's important,' writes David Huckvale, '[...] is not, after all, archaeological **authenticity**, but exotically Egyptian **effect**.'[252] The Egyptian Gothic tell us next to nothing about Egypt's culture or religion. These stories tell us about the storytellers, and about their audiences: about ourselves.

Pyramids of Mars relies closely on its cinematic ancestors, especially Hammer's *The Mummy*, and it tells the same tale as they do of fascination and fear. But it stands out for two reasons. Firstly, it insists on a scientific basis for everything in the story. This is the inverse of the movies, in which the supernatural is real and you doubt its power at your peril. And secondly, the show-makers have not just consulted real Egyptian mythology, they've used it as the basis of the story. This is not just a struggle for survival by a small group of tomb violators; it's a battle of literally cosmic proportions. The characters and events in *Pyramids* have recognisable predecessors in fiction, but Sutekh is unique. In the movies, the gods only appear as idols, as images. Sutekh is alive and present.

In a review in Locus[253], Russell Letson writes that 'Charles Stross's Laundry series[254] belongs to a long line of attempts to rationalize or otherwise repackage and domesticate the supernatural',

---

[251] Lupton, '"Mummymania" for the Masses', p36.
[252] Huckvale, *Touchstones of Gothic Horror*, p187.
[253] Letson, Russell, 'Locus Looks at Books'. *Locus* 77 (1).
[254] Starting with *The Atrocity Archives* (2004).

comparing the novels to tales of 'occult detectives (paleo-Ghostbusters)' such as William Hope Hodgson's Thomas Carnacki[255]. Although the **Laundry Files** books are very different in style and content to *Pyramids*, they share a premise with **Doctor Who** old and new: the supernatural is in fact scientific, and can even be harnessed as technology: the petrifying gaze of Medusa can be delivered through a camera. Sutekh uses technology which any advanced alien might have – robots, a computer database, the time tunnel – and even his seemingly paranormal powers can be disrupted by a radio-jamming signal. Of Stross's series, Letson remarks that it:

> 'feels like an attempt to hold Something at arm's length – to domesticate, rationalise, encyst, or cushion the raw material of terror and fear; to embed it in a seriocomic adventure in which our viewpoint character and a few others survive the carnage.'

He could well be describing **Doctor Who**.

Is this desire to rationalise the irrational a flaw? In **Doctor Who**, there are many virtues, but none is higher than rationality, expressed in the form of the Doctor's scientific knowledge. Perhaps this is why it's immoral to exploit *The Mutants*' Solonians, whose culture has been destroyed by invaders, but acceptable to do so to the Uxarians in *Colony in Space*[256] and the Exxilons in *Death to the*

---

[255] Thomas Carnacki is an occult detective created by William Hope Hodgson for a series of short stories published between 1910 and 1912.
[256] Orthia, 'Sociopathetic Abscess', p6.

Daleks: the latter two civilisations have degenerated, losing science and becoming superstitious.

As a champion of science, the Doctor consistently opposes what he sees as its misuse, frequently confronting scientists from the villainous (Davros) to the frankly bonkers (Zaroff[257]) to the merely misguided: as he reminds Professor Kettlewell in *Robot*, 'in science, as in morality, the end never justifies the means'. Perhaps this is why the Doctor does not hesitate to make poison gas in an attempt to kill both the mad scientist Solon and the monster-tyrant Morbius. Having made immoral use of science, it's only appropriate that the contents of Solon's own laboratory are used against him.

It may be misused, but **Doctor Who** is consistently optimistic about science itself. It's the reason that **Doctor Who** never frightened me as a child, while **The Goodies** (BBC 1970-1980, ITV 1981-1982), shown beforehand on the Australian television network ABC, was sometimes terrifying. More than once, the comedy adventures of Graeme, Bill, and Tim – often triggered by their ridiculous scientific experiments – ended with their (temporary) demise. The Doctor faced terrors, but his reason and knowledge, or at least his technology, will always win through in the end.

The Impossible Planet / The Satan Pit, the descendant of *Pyramids of Mars*, directly addresses the Doctor's relationship with rationality and science. While Sutekh has merely been imprisoned for millennia, the Beast claims to have been trapped since 'before time', a serious challenge to the Doctor's understanding of how time works. The Doctor quickly recognises Sutekh; the Beast comes as a shock. The Doctor uses reason to calm the superstitious fears

---

[257] *The Underwater Menace* (1967).

of the Sanctuary Base's crew and to challenge the claims of the Beast to be the Devil ('There's more religions than there are planets in the sky [...] Which devil are you?'[258]), and finally to solve the puzzle of its prison, but it takes more than this to save the day; his faith in Rose's agency is critical to the Beast's defeat.

But once again there's a disturbing undercurrent to this happy ending. With time to make only one trip before planet and base plunge into the black hole, the Doctor saves one human – his fellow scientist, Ida – and leaves 50 or more of the humans' slaves to die. In *Pyramids* and even in *The Brain of Morbius*, the Doctor's seeming callousness is appropriate to the urgency of the situation. Here it's harder to understand.

Doctor Who fans look to the Doctor as a model of correct moral behaviour and can be outraged when he fails to live up to the standards we expect of him. In this, perhaps we're mistaken. Sutekh is all-powerful and all-evil; nothing the Doctor does to oppose him could possibly be wrong. But the threat of Sutekh's escape is an exceptional situation. Other stories suggest that the Doctor's actions are guided as much by his beliefs **about** reason and science as they are by reason and science – including his belief that, as a rational scientist, he knows what's best.

'Your Evil Is My Good'

While Sutekh is all-powerful and all-evil, the Egyptian god Set is a much more complicated character. He is a murderer and a villain, but he is also a protector of the cosmos, and even a clown. By contrast with later religions, which insist – sometimes violently – on

---

[258] *The Satan Pit.*

a single, definitive understanding of the divine, Egyptian myth readily accommodated conflicting ideas which to us look like internal contradictions: illogical, irrational. Did Re create the universe, or was it Atum, or Amun, or Neith? These stories were not in competition; they were appropriate at different times, in different places, and sat comfortably shoulder-to-shoulder. There was sacrilege – tomb-robbing, for example – but there was no heresy[259]. Claude Traunecker writes that because the truth of the divine was not accessible to human beings, then different attempts to approach it were valid:

> 'This **multiplicity of approaches** permitted the juxtaposition of apparently contradictory images. Thus, it did not matter whether the truth of the sky was contained in the image of a celestial river on which the sun barque sailed, in the image of a woman's body giving birth to the sun each morning, or in the image of the star-covered belly of a cow whose legs supported the sky.'[260]

Growing up with the ABC's constant repeats of **Doctor Who**, I was never troubled by the frequent failure of the special effects to look realistic. It didn't matter that, when Sutekh sends the TARDIS key through the time tunnel and into Scarman's hands, it's obviously dangling from strings; what mattered was that Sutekh had control over the Doctor and the TARDIS. When I was a little older, I remember thinking the show could be seen as a dramatisation of

---

[259] Except perhaps the famous example of Akhenaten, the father of Tutankhamun, who suppressed the worship of gods other than his own sun-god, the Aten. Even this was a matter of official state religion rather than orthodox belief.

[260] Traunecker, Claude, *The Gods of Egypt*, p11.

real events. Obviously, the strings weren't there when Sutekh **really** sent the key through. It was a useful way to excuse internal contradictions, errors of science and history, and other blemishes: the TV show was only an attempt to approach the truth of the original – so that multiple, seemingly incompatible attempts were all valid. Later still I could see how this could be applied to **Doctor Who** beyond the small screen. Novels, comics, audios, and so on, are all efforts to reach some basic truth – most importantly, I think, about the nature of the Doctor himself – which none of them can ever precisely define. Perhaps the Egyptians' 'multiplicity of approaches' could be a useful alternative approach for a fandom obsessed with continuity and canonicity.

BIBLIOGRAPHY

Books

Asimov, Isaac, *Extraterrestrial Civilizations*. New York, Fawcett Columbine, 1979. ISBN 9780307792303.

Binder, Eando (Earl Andrew Binder and Otto Binder), *Puzzle of the Space Pyramids*. New York, Curtis, 1971.

Bleeker, CJ, *Hathor and Thoth: Two Key Figures of the Ancient Egyptian Religion*. Leiden, Brill, 1973. ISBN 9789004037342.

Boothby, Guy, *Pharos, the Egyptian*. London, Ward Lock & Co, 1899.

Bucher-Jones, Simon, *Image of the Fendahl*. **The Black Archive** #5. Edinburgh, Obverse Books, 2016. ISBN 9781909031418.

Butler, David, ed, *Time and Relative Dissertations in Space: Critical Perspectives on Doctor Who*. Manchester and New York, Manchester University Press, 2007. ISBN 9780719076824.

> Murray, Andy, 'The Talons of Robert Holmes'.

> Rafer, David, 'Mythic Identity in **Doctor Who**'.

Campbell, Mark, *Doctor Who*. **The Pocket Essential**. Harpenden, Pocket Essentials, 2000. ISBN 9781903047194.

Cardin, Matt, ed, *Mummies around the Word: An Encyclopedia of Mummies in History, Religion and Popular Culture*. Santa Barbara CA, ABC-CLIO, 2014. ISBN 9781610694193.

Carruthers, William, ed, *Histories of Egyptology: Interdisciplinary Measures*. New York, Routledge, 2014. ISBN 9780415843690.

Day, Jasmine, 'Repeating Death: The High Priest Character in Mummy Horror Films'

Daly, Nicholas, *Modernism, Romance, and the Fin de Siècle: Popular Fiction and British Culture, 1880-1914*. New York, Cambridge University Press, 1999. ISBN 9780521641036.

Davies, Russell T, and Benjamin Cook, *The Writer's Tale: The Final Chapter*. London, BBC Books, 2010. ISBN 9781846078613.

Day, Jasmine, *The Mummy's Curse: Mummymania in the English-speaking World*. London, Routledge, 2006. ISBN 9780415340229.

Dennis, Jonathan, *Ghost Light*. **The Black Archive** #6. Edinburgh, Obverse Books, 2016. ISBN 9781909031432.

Dicks, Terrance, *Doctor Who and the Pyramids of Mars*. **The Target Doctor Who Library** #50. London, WH Allen, 1976. ISBN 9780426200772.

Douglass, Ellsworth, *Pharaoh's Broker*. London, CA Pearson, 1899.

Doyle, Arthur Conan. 'The Ring of Thoth.' *The Captain of the Pole Star and Other Tales*. London, Longmans Green & Co, 1890.

Du Maurier, George, *Trilby*. Leipzig, Bernhard Tauchnitz, 1894.

Dynes, Wayne R, and Stephen Donaldson, eds, *Homosexuality in the Ancient World*. New York, London, Garland, 1992. ISBN 9780815305460.

Edwards, IES, *Tutankhamun, His Tomb and Its Treasures*. New York, Metropolitan Museum of Art and Alfred A Knopf, 1977. ISBN 9780394411705.

Faulkner, Raymond O, *The Ancient Egyptian Coffin Texts*, Volume 1. Warminster, Aris and Phillips, 1973. ISBN 9780856680052.

Faulkner, Raymond O, *The Ancient Egyptian Pyramid Texts*. Oxford, Clarendon Press, 1969. ISBN 9780198154372.

Faulkner, Raymond O, *A Concise Dictionary of Middle Egyptian*. 1962. Oxford, Griffith Institute, 2006.

Frazer, Sir James George, *The Golden Bough: A Study in Magic and Religion*. 1890. New York, Macmillan, 1922.

Griffiths, J Gwyn, *The Conflict of Horus and Seth from Egyptian and Classical Sources*. Liverpool, Liverpool University Press, 1960. ISBN 9780853230717.

Guirand, Felix, ed, *New Larousse Encyclopedia of Mythology*. London and New York, Hamlyn, 1968. ISBN 9780600023517.

Guirand, Felix, ed, *Larousse Encyclopedia of Mythology*. London, Batchworth Press, 1959. ISBN 9780765193841.

Haggard, H Rider, *She: A History of Adventure*. London, Longmans Green & Co, 1887.

Haining, Peter, *The Mummy: Stories of the Living Corpse*. New York, Severn House, 1988. ISBN 9789994022151.

Hansen, Christopher J, *Ruminations, Peregrinations, and Regenerations: A Critical Approach to Doctor Who*. Newcastle upon Tyne, Cambridge Scholars Publishing, 2010. ISBN 9781443820844.

Vasquez, Joshua, 'The Moral Economy of **Doctor Who**: Forgiving Fans and the Objects of their Devotion'.

Haywood, John, *The Penguin Historical Atlas of Ancient Civilizations*. Penguin Books, London, 2005. ISBN 9780141014487.

Hogan, David J, *Dark Romance: Sexuality in the Horror Film*. Jefferson NC, Mcfarland, 1986. ISBN 9780899501901.

Hornung, Erik, *The Ancient Egyptian Books of the Afterlife*. David Lorton, trans, Ithaca NY, Cornell University Press, 1999. ISBN 9780801485152.

Hornung, Erik, *Idea into Image: Essays on Ancient Egyptian Thought*. New York, Timken, 1992. ISBN 9780943221113.

Howe, David J, Mark Stammers and Stephen James Walker, *Doctor Who: The Eighties*. London, Virgin Publishing, 1997. ISBN 9780753501283.

Howe, David J, Mark Stammers and Stephen James Walker, *The First Doctor*. **Doctor Who: The Handbook**. London, Virgin Publishing, 1994. ISBN 9780426204301.

Huckvale, David, *Touchstones of Gothic Horror: A Film Genealogy of Eleven Motifs and Images*. Jefferson NC, McFarland, 2010. ISBN 9780786447824.

Johnson, Tom, *Censored Screams: The British Ban on Hollywood Horror in the Thirties*. Jefferson NC, McFarland, 1997. ISBN 9780786403943.

Johnson, Tom, and Mark A Miller, *The Christopher Lee Filmography: All Theatrical Releases, 1948-2003*. Jefferson NC and London, McFarland, 2004. ISBN 9780786446919.

Joshi, ST, *Icons of Horror and the Supernatural*, Volume 1. Westport CT and London, Greenwood Press, 2007. ISBN 9780313337819.

Kemp, Barry, *How to Read the Egyptian Book of the Dead*. New York and London, Norton, 2007. ISBN 9780393330793.

Lacovara, Peter, *The World of Ancient Egypt: A Daily Life Encyclopedia*. Volume II. Santa Barbara CA, ABC-CLIO, 2017. ISBN 9781440845840.

Leitz, Christian, *Lexikon der Ägyptischen Götter und Götterbezeichnungen*. Dudley MA, Peeters, 2002-03. ISBN 9789042911468.

Lichtheim, Miriam, *Ancient Egyptian Literature Volume III: The Late Period*. Berkeley, Los Angeles and London, University of California Press, 2006. ISBN 9780520248441.

Luckhurst, Roger, *The Mummy's Curse: The True History of a Dark Fantasy*. Oxford, Oxford University Press, 2012. ISBN 9780199698714.

MacDonald, Sally, and Michael Rice, eds, *Consuming Ancient Egypt*. London, University College London, 2003. ISBN 9781598747577.

Lupton, Carter, '"Mummymania"' for the masses': Is Egyptology Cursed by the Mummy's Curse?

Marsh, Richard. *The Beetle: A Mystery*. London, Skeffington & Son, 1897.

Mercer, Samuel AB, *Horus: Royal God of Egypt*. Society of Oriental Research, Grafton MA, 1942.

Mitchell, Timothy, *Colonising Egypt*. Cambridge, New York, Melbourne, Cambridge University Press, 1988. ISBN 9780521334488.

Newman, Kim, *BFI TV Classics: Doctor Who*. London, British Film Institute Publishing, 2005. ISBN 9781844570904.

Orman, Kate, *Set Piece*. **Doctor Who: The New Adventures**. London, Virgin Publishing Ltd, 1995. ISBN 9780426204367.

Petrie, WM Flinders, and JE Quibell, *Naqada and Ballas*. London: B Quaritch, 1895.

Pinch, Geraldine, *Egyptian Mythology*. Santa Barbara CA, ABC-CLIO, 2002. ISBN 9780195170245.

Pixley, Andrew, *Ace of Wands: Viewing Notes*. Lea Valley, Network Distributing, 2007. No ISBN.

Plutarch, *Moralia*. Frank C Babbitt, trans, Cambridge MA, Harvard University Press, 1936.

Potts, DT, ed, *A Companion to the Archaeology of the Ancient Near East*. Oxford, Wiley-Blackwell, 2012. ISBN 9781405189880.

    Magee, Peter, 'The Foundations of Antiquities Departments'.

Price, Campbell, Roger Forshaw, Andrew Chamberlain and Paul Nicholson, eds, *Mummies, Magic and Medicine: Multidisciplinary Essays for Rosalie David*. Manchester, Manchester University Press, 2016. ISBN 9781784992439.

    Turner, Philip J, 'Thoughts on Seth the conman'.

Rohmer, Sax (Arthur Henry Ward), *The Mystery of Dr Fu-Manchu*. 1913. *The Insidious Dr Fu-Manchu*, New York, Dover, 1997. ISBN 9781306366946.

Rohmer, Sax (Arthur Henry Ward), *The Green Eyes of Bast*. New York: RM McBride, 1920.

Serviss, Garrett P, *Edison's Conquest of Mars*. 1898. Burlington Ontario, Apogee Books, 2005. ISBN 9780973820300.

Shafer, Byron Esel, ed, *Religion in Ancient Egypt: Gods, Myths, and Personal Practice*. Ithaca NY and London, Cornell University Press, 1991. ISBN 9780801425509.

Shaw, Ian, *The Oxford History of Ancient Egypt*. Oxford, Oxford University Press, 2000. ISBN 9780198150343.

Shermer, Michael, ed, *The Skeptic Encyclopedia of Pseudoscience*, Volume One. Santa Barbara CA, ABC-CLIO, 2002. ISBN 9781576076538.

Silverman, David P, *Ancient Egypt*. New York, Oxford University Press, 1997. ISBN 9780195219524.

Simpson, William Kelly. *The Literature of Ancient Egypt: An Anthology of Stories, Instructions, and Poetry*. New Haven CT and London, Yale University Press, 1972. ISBN 9780300014822.

Stoker, Bram, *Dracula*. London, Archibald Constable and Co, 1897.

Stoker, Bram. *The Jewel of Seven Stars*. London, William Heinemann, 1903.

Szpakowska, Kasia Maria, *Behind Closed Eyes: Dreams and Nightmares in Ancient Egypt*. Swansea, Classical Press of Wales, 2003. ISBN 9780954384500.

Te Velde, Herman, *Seth: God of Confusion*. Leiden, EJ Brill, 1967. ISBN 9789004054028.

Traunecker, Claude. *The Gods of Egypt*. David Lorton, trans, Ithaca NY and London, Cornell University Press, 2001. ISBN 9780801438349.

Von Däniken, Erich, *Chariots of the Gods? Unsolved Mysteries of the Past*. Michael Heron, trans, London and Toronto, Souvenir Press and Ryerson Press, 1969. ISBN 9780285502567.

Weinbaum, Stanley G, *A Martian Odyssey and Others*. Reading PA, Fantasy Press, 1949.

Wells, HG, *The War of the Worlds*. London, William Heinemann, 1897.

Whewell, William, *The Plurality of Worlds: An Essay*. London, Parker and Son, 1853.

Wilde, Sir William Robert, *Narrative of a Voyage to Madeira, Teneriffe, and Along the Shores of the Mediterranean*. Dublin, William Curry Jr and Co, 1844.

Wilkinson, Richard H, *Reading Egyptian Art: A Hieroglyphic Guide to Ancient Egyptian Painting and Sculpture*. London, Thames and Hudson, 1992. ISBN 9780500277515.

Wilkinson, Richard H, *Symbol and Magic in Egyptian Art*. London, Thames and Hudson, 1994. ISBN 9780500280706.

Periodicals

Doctor Who Magazine (DWM). Marvel UK, Panini, BBC, 1979-.

'Overseas Overview', DWM #71, cover date December 1982.

Barnes, Alan. 'The Fact of Fiction: Image of the Fendahl'. DWM #379, cover date February 2007.

Bignell, Richard, 'The Missing Stories'. DWM #198, cover date April 1993.

Pixley, Andrew, 'Archive: Pyramids of Mars'. DWM #300, cover date February 2001.

Pixley, Andrew, 'Pyramids of Mars: Archive Extra'. DWM Special Edition #8, cover date September 2004.

Pixley, Andrew, 'Archive: The Celestial Toymaker'. DWM #196, cover date February 1993.

Russell, Gary, 'Interview: Robert Holmes'. DWM #100, cover date May 1985.

Fortean Times (FT). Various, now Dennis Publishing Ltd, 1973-.

Cornell, Paul, 'Doctor Who: Forteana in Time and Space'. FT #218, September 2014.

'Letters: Pyramids on Mars'. FT #320, November 2014.

Journal of the American Research Center in Egypt (JARCE). Boston, The Center, 1962-.

Cruz-Uribe, Eugene, 'Sth ꜣ phty: "Seth, God of Power and Might"'. JARCE #45, 2009.

Te Velde, Herman, 'The Egyptian God Seth as a Trickster'. JARCE #7, 1968.

'At the Dublin Theatre Festival', *Punch*, 19 October 1966, issue 6580.

'Cinemas', *The Guardian* (Manchester), 20 February 1971.

'Space Economies'. *The Canberra Times*, 17 January 1970.

Arata, Stephen D, 'The Occidental Tourist: *Dracula* and the Anxiety of Reverse Colonization'. *Victorian Studies* 33(4). Bloomington IN, Indiana University Press, 1990.

Borghouts, JF, 'The Evil Eye of Apophis'. *Journal of Egyptian Archaeology* 59. London, The Egypt Exploration Society, 1973.

Bulfin, Ailise, 'The Fiction of Gothic Egypt and British Imperial Paranoia: The Curse of the Suez Canal'. *English Literature in Transition, 1880-1920* 54(4). Greensboro NC, ELT Press, 2011.

Cavendish, Richard, ed, 'Horns'. *Man, Myth, and Magic: an Illustrated Encyclopedia of the Supernatural*. Purnell for BPC Publishing, 1970.

Cooper, Guy H, 'Coyote in Navajo Religion and Cosmology'. *The Canadian Journal of Native Studies* VII 2, 1987.

Letson, Russell, 'Locus Looks at Books'. Locus 77(1). San Leandro CA, Locus Publications, July 2016.

Musch, Sebastian, 'The Atomic Priesthood and Nuclear Waste Management-Religion: Religion, Sci-fi Literature and the End of our Civilization'. *Zygon: Journal of Religion and Science* 51(3), Chicago, University of Chicago Press, 2016.

Orthia, Lindy, 'Sociopathetic Abscess or Yawning Chasm? The Absent Postcolonial Transition in **Doctor Who**'. *The Journal of Commonwealth Literature*, 45 (2). London, Heinemann Educational Books and University of Leeds, June 2010.

Parker, RA, 'Ancient Egyptian Astronomy'. *Philosophical Transactions of the Royal Society of London*. Series A, Mathematical and Physical Sciences, 276 (1257). London, Royal Society Publishing, May 2, 1974.

Ulmer, Rivka B Kern, 'The Divine Eye in Ancient Egypt and in the Midrashic Interpretation of Formative Judaism'. *Journal of Religion an Society* #5. Omaha, Kripke Center, 2003.

Television

Ace of Wands. Thames Television, 1970-72.

> *The Power of Atep*, 1972

Blake's 7. BBC, 1978-1981.

> *Sarcophagus*, 1980.

Doctor Who. BBC, 1963-.

The Goodies. BBC 1970-80, ITV 1981-82.

Mystery and Imagination. ABC Weekend Television, Thames Television, 1966-70.

> *Curse of the Mummy*, 1970.

The Power of the Witch. BBC, 1971.

The Sarah Jane Adventures. BBC, 2007-11.

> *The Wedding of Sarah Jane Smith*, 2009.

Sexton Blake and the Demon God. BBC, 1978.

The Tomorrow People. Thames Television, 1973-79.

> *Slaves of Jedikiah*, 1973

> *Worlds Away*, 1975

Film

Cabanne, Christy, dir, *The Mummy's Hand*. Universal Studios, 1940.

Carreras, Michael, dir, *The Curse of the Mummy's Tomb*. Hammer Film Productions, 1964.

Fisher, Terence, dir, *The Mummy*. Hammer Film Productions, 1959.

Freund, Karl, dir, *The Mummy*. Universal Studios, 1932.

Gilling, John, dir, *The Mummy's Shroud*, Hammer Film Productions, 1967.

Goodwins, Leslie, dir, *The Mummy's Curse*. Universal Studios, 1944.

Holt, Seth, dir, *Blood from the Mummy's Tomb*, Hammer Film Productions, 1971.

Lamont, Charles, dir, *Abbott and Costello Meet the Mummy*. Universal Studios, 1955.

Le Borg, Reginald, dir, *The Mummy's Ghost*. Universal Studios, 1944.

Rivas, Ray, dir, *UFOs: Past, Present, and Future*. Sandler Institutional Films, 1974.

Sharp, Don, dir, *The Brides of Fu Manchu*. Constantin Film, 1966.

Thomas, Gerald, dir, *Carry on Screaming!* Peter Rogers Productions, 1966.

Young, Harold, dir, *The Mummy's Tomb*. Universal Studios, 1942.

Web

'BBC Genome Project'. http://genome.ch.bbc.co.uk/. Accessed 1 April 2017.

'Irish actor Peter Mayock as The Young Lieutenant in a scene…'. RTE Archive. https://stillslibrary.rte.ie/indexplus/image/1023/057.html. Accessed 13 December 2016.

'Stargrove'. Hampshire Gardens Trust, August 2009. http://research.hgt.org.uk/item/stargrove/. Accessed 15 November 2016.

'Vic Tablian', Internet Movie Database. http://www.imdb.com/name/nm0846004/. Accessed 13 December 2016.

'A Vignette from the Book of the Dead of Lady Cheritwebeshet'. Getty Images. http://www.gettyimages.com.au/detail/news-photo/vignette-from-the-book-of-the-dead-of-lady-cheritwebeshet-news-photo/152203173. Accessed 13 December 2016.

'Autonomous Weapons: An Open Letter from AI & Robotics Researchers'. Future of Life Institute, 28 July 2016. http://futureoflife.org/open-letter-autonomous-weapons/. Accessed 16 December 2016.

'Gale Artemis: Primary Sources'. http://gale.cengage.co.uk/gale-artemis/gale-artemis-primary-sources.aspx. Accessed 13 February 2017.

'Gilded Outer Coffin of Henutmehyt'. British Museum. http://culturalinstitute.britishmuseum.org/asset-viewer/gilded-outer-coffin-of-henutmehyt/PgFbOqXe_29Cxw?hl=en. Accessed 28 December 2016.

Boothby, Guy, *Pharos, the Egyptian*. 1899. Ebooks@Adelaide, University of Adelaide.

https://ebooks.adelaide.edu.au/b/boothby/guy/pharos-the-egyptian/. Accessed 28 October 2016.

Ciechanowski, Walt, and Andrew Peregrine, *The Fourth Doctor Sourcebook* (Doctor Who: Adventures in Time and Space role-playing game). Cubicle 7 Entertainment, 2014. http://cubicle7.co.uk/wp-content/uploads/2014/02/The-Fourth-Doctor-Pyramids-of-Mars-Web.pdf. Accessed 16 December 2016.

Conca, James, 'Talking to the Future – Hey, There's Nuclear Waste Buried Here!'. Forbes, 17 April 2015. http://www.forbes.com/sites/jamesconca/2015/04/17/talking-to-the-future-hey-theres-nuclear-waste-buried-here/. Accessed 29 December 2016.

Douglass, Ellsworth, *Pharaoh's Broker*. 1899. Project Gutenberg ebook. https://www.gutenberg.org/ebooks/25295. Accessed 10 February 2017.

Douros, George. Unicode Fonts for Ancient Scripts. http://users.teilar.gr/~g1951d/. Accessed 4 February 2013.

Doyle, Arthur Conan. 'The Ring of Thoth.' 1890. *The Captain of the Pole Star and Other Tales*. Project Gutenberg ebook. http://www.gutenberg.org/ebooks/294. Accessed 10 February 2017.

Doyle, Arthur Conan. 'Lot No 249.' 1892. Wikisource. https://en.wikisource.org/wiki/Lot_No._249. Accessed 14 February 2017.

Frazer, Sir James George, *The Golden Bough: A Study in Magic and Religion*. Bartleby.com, 2000. http://www.bartleby.com/196/. Accessed 14 December 2016.

Freeman, David, 'Mars "Pyramid" Seen By NASA Rover Isn't Quite What It Seems'. *The Huffington Post*, 26 July 2015. http://www.huffingtonpost.com.au/entry/mars-pyramid-nasa-curiosity-rover-video_n_7665080. Accessed 13 December 2016.

Ghigo, F, 'Pre-History of Radio Astronomy'. National Radio Astronomy Observatory, 27 March 2003. http://www.nrao.edu/whatisra/hist_prehist.shtml. Accessed 15 November 2016.

Haggard, H Rider, *She*. Project Gutenberg ebook. http://www.gutenberg.org/ebooks/3155. Accessed 8 November 2016.

Kmtsesh, 'What's up with Mummies?'. Ancient Near East - Just The Facts, 9 September 2012. https://ancientneareast.org/2012/09/09/whats-up-with-mummies/. Accessed 15 December 2016.

Marsh, Richard. *The Beetle: a Mystery*. 1897. Project Gutenberg ebook. http://www.gutenberg.org/ebooks/5164. Accessed 10 February 2017.

Moneim, Moataz Abdel, 'The Last of Egypt's Tarboush Makers'. *Asharq al-Awsat*, 28 February 2014. http://english.aawsat.com/2014/02/article55329409/the-last-of-egypts-tarboush-makers. Accessed 15 December 2016.

Petrie, WM Flinders, and JE Quibell, *Naqada and Ballas*. London, B Quaritch, 1895.

https://archive.org/download/cu31924028748261/cu31924028748261.pdf. Accessed 12 May 2016.

Plutarch, *Moralia*. Frank C Babbitt, trans. http://penelope.uchicago.edu/Thayer/e/roman/texts/plutarch/moralia/isis_and_osiris*/home. Accessed 7 August 2016.

Rohmer, Sax (Arthur Henry Ward), *The Green Eyes of Bast*. 1920. Project Gutenberg ebook. http://www.gutenberg.org/ebooks/15323. Accessed 2 December 2016.

Serviss, Garrett P, *Edison's Conquest of Mars*. 1898. Project Gutenberg ebook. http://www.gutenberg.org/ebooks/19141. Accessed 25 October 2016.

Sheehan, William, 'Appendix 1: Oppositions of Mars, 1901-2035', 2 February 1997. https://www.uapress.arizona.edu/onlinebks/MARS/APPENDS.HTM. Accessed 13 December 2016.

Stoker, Bram, *Dracula*. 1897. Project Gutenberg ebook. https://www.gutenberg.org/ebooks/345. Accessed 7 November 2016.

Stoker, Bram. *The Jewel of Seven Stars*. 1903. Project Gutenberg ebook. http://www.gutenberg.org/ebooks/3781. Accessed 7 November 2016.

Weinbaum, Stanley Grauman, 'A Martian Odyssey'. 1949. Project Gutenberg ebook. http://www.gutenberg.org/ebooks/23731. Accessed 29 December 2016.

Weinbaum, Stanley Grauman, 'Valley of Dreams'. 1949. Project Gutenberg ebook. http://www.gutenberg.org/ebooks/22301. Accessed 23 September 2016.

Wells, HG, *The War of the Worlds*. 1897. Project Gutenberg ebook.
https://www.gutenberg.org/ebooks/36. Accessed 16 December
2016.

Whewell, William, *The Plurality of Worlds: An Essay*. London, Parker
and Son, 1853.
https://archive.org/details/ofpluralityofwor00whewuoft. Accessed
2 January 2017.

Wilde, Sir William Robert, *Narrative of a Voyage to Madeira,
Teneriffe and Along the Shores of the Mediterranean*. 1844.
https://archive.org/details/narrativeavoyag01wildgoog. Accessed
29 December 2016.

BIOGRAPHY

Kate Orman is best known for writing numerous **Doctor Who** novels, many with her co-author and husband Jonathan Blum. She continues to publish original science fiction and fantasy. Kate has been hooked on Ancient Egypt since she was a young child, when she first encountered its fascinating hieroglyphic writing and numberless gods. Visit her blog at kateorman.wordpress.com.